BUILDING BETTER SCHOOLS BY
ENGAGING
SUPPORT STAFF

SAM BARTLETT &
VIE HERLOCKER

www.engageinstitute.com/buildingbetterschools

© 2007 ENGAGE! Press
Printed and bound in the United States of America

ENGAGE! Press
411 N. Main Street
Galax, VA 24333

This book contains information gathered from many sources. The printer, publisher, and author disclaim any personal liability, either directly or indirectly, for advice or information presented within. Although the author, publisher, and printer have used care and diligence in the presentation, and made every effort to ensure the accuracy and completeness of the information contained in this book, we assume no responsibility for errors, inaccuracies, omissions, or any inconsistency herein.

First Printing 2007
ISBN No. 978–0–9814543–0–6
Library of Congress Cataloging–in–Publication Data

Dedication

This book is dedicated to my mom and dad, Bill and Nell Bartlett, and to my father and mother–in–law, Jack and Claudia Jalo. You live in a manner worthy of others to follow.
—Sam

This book is dedicated to my husband, Lee. You are my greatest supporter and encourager. GHY! And to my sister, Susan Stallings Alberta. Your enthusiasm, your ready smile, your determination, and your unselfish heart continue to inspire me. You are my hero.
—Vie

Acknowledgments

I recently pulled a muscle in my lower back helping a friend move. I was laid up for a couple of days, and my team at Family Friendly Schools sent flowers in a pink boot (I am a cowboy at heart who rides and trains horses) with this note: "We didn't know you could pull muscles you do not have." This is a glimpse of what it is like to work with some incredible people. Thanks, Steve, Deb, Danny, Joan, and Vie for knowing when and how to push me hard and for picking up the slack when I get off track. Your fingerprints are all over this book. Vie is a coauthor's dream.

Larson's Lodge advertises on billboards all over the state of Florida with this tagline: "We treat you like family, probably better!" No one treats me better or is more important to me than my family. To Linda, my wife of twenty–six years, and our five children: Curtis, Bethany, Faith, Caleb, and Victoria. Thanks for teaching me the meaning of love. Your unconditional support has given me the freedom to take risks in life, knowing that whatever happens we have one another.

A final thanks to those who have shaped my development. My philosophy of education has been significantly influenced by Dr. Larry Rowedder, Mike Rutherford, Kathy Kennedy, Dr. Bill Harrison, Jerry King, Suzanne Hall, Dr. Steve Constantino, Deb Holton, and thousands of educators (including support staff) who have attended my seminars and shared lessons learned in the trenches. My spiritual mentors have taught me to hold material things loosely in my hands and to hold God and others close to my heart. Thanks to Jim Hebel, Dr. Don Joy, Sylvia Ball, Joe Healey, Steve Somers, Brent Sapp, Mike Dinkins, and my church family at Cornerstone Community. Nick Davis, Steve Roche, and Rogers Kirven have patiently counseled me on how to run a business and have been there when I have struggled. I will honor all of you by investing in others as you have invested in me. Together we can liberate greatness!

—Sam

Thank you, Sam, for the privilege of collaborating with you on this project. Your enthusiasm and optimism are contagious, and your ability to see opportunities in every obstacle enlarged my vision as well. I found myself saying, "If Sam believes it can be done, then I believe it can be done." You are an inspirational teacher whose lessons will go with me far beyond this project.

Thank you, Steve Constantino, for sharing your poem.

Thank you, Joan Gillespie, for your encouragement, friendship, laughter, and for always helping me with the office machines.

Thank you, Danny Hafner, techno-guru and graphic designer, for making our manuscript a book. I appreciate your patience, assistance, and advice. Thank you, also, to your wife, Carey, and children Lake and Skylar for being so understanding of the long hours spent at the office.

Thank you, Deb Holton, for advising, editing, and checking details — over and over and over. You and Danny could both be included as co-writers on this book.

Thank you, Kathy Ide, for the editorial assistance and excellent suggestions.

Thank you to my sons and daughter-in-law, Nathan, Catherine, and Justin, for always believing in me.

Thank you, to my writing group, "The Sis-Duhs." Your prayers and feedback get me through every project.

Thank you, Floyd, our four-footed office guardian angel.

—Vie

Contents

Section 1:

Ambassadors and Professionals

CHAPTER ONE

FROM "OTHER" TO AMBASSADOR

*The will to win, the desire to succeed, the urge to reach your full potential...
these are the keys that will unlock the door to personal excellence.*
— *Eddie Robinson*

For the last twenty years, I have crisscrossed the country presenting seminars for schools, Fortune 500 companies, and governmental agencies. A few months ago, I was speaking on Sizzling Customer Service to a group of custodians and maintenance workers from a Northeastern school district. At the end of the day, participants completed an evaluation form.

A man in the back of the room asked me to come to his table. I hurried over, thinking he might need some clarification on filling out the form. Instead, he shocked me with these words: "Mr. Bartlett, this form reflects how I sometimes believe maintenance workers are valued by our leadership. It asks us to check the box beside our position in the district. But do you see custodians? We're not even on the list. The only box we can check is 'other.' You have been saying all day that we are important, that we are ambassadors, that we are professionals. If this is true, why aren't we on the list?"

I thought about this man's comment on the long flight home, and before the plane touched down in Charlotte, North Carolina, I knew I had to write a book for support staff. I had to spread the message that you are not an "other." You are a hidden hero and are in a position to become an Engaged Ambassador for your school system. You are an important member of the educational team and a crucial member of your community.

Do you know where the public gets most of its information about schools? From the newspaper? From the principal's weekly parent bulletin? From the teachers? From the students? The correct answer is "none of the above."

A few years ago, the National School Public Relations Association reported that the public gets most of its information about schools from the support staff, in this order:

1. Secretaries
2. Custodians
3. Bus drivers
4. Cafeteria workers

You are an ambassador for your school or district. You are out there in the community. You go to the ball games. You shop in the local stores. It is only natural that your neighbors, friends at church and clubs, your hairdresser, and others you meet will ask about your job. You are a major source of information. You are in a position to be an Engaged Ambassador—a communicator of good will between the public and your district.

I invite you to join me on a journey as we integrate proven principles of providing Sizzling Customer Service with powerful stories from twenty–one support staff members. These men and women are making a difference in the educational mission of their school districts—and so can you!

CHAPTER TWO

WANTED: PROFESSIONALS. AMATEURS NEED NOT APPLY.

Professionalism is as much or more an attitude as it is a skill level.
—Richard Huggins

You are probably shaking your head at the chapter title. You think a professional needs a college degree with a string of letters following his name. Well, let me tell you about my father. My father has been a truck driver most of his life and is one of my heroes because of his work ethic and because he has never stopped learning. Although I have a lot more formal education, his large dose of common sense frequently makes him the teacher and me the student. He is a true professional and can maneuver an eighteen–wheeler in a tight spot as masterfully as Tiger Woods can get a little ball to fall into a tiny hole. He laughs aloud watching me attempt to back my horse trailer into the shed. After a few tries he gets a smirk on his face and yells out, "You'd better get out and let a professional do it. We don't have time for amateurs. We're going to be here all day."

The *American Heritage Dictionary* defines a professional as (1) a person following a profession, especially a learned profession; (2) one who earns a living in a given or implied occupation; and (3) a skilled practitioner; an expert. I like to think of professionals as those who are experts in what they do; those who have enthusiasm for their work and pride in doing it well; those who are paid for their knowledge and skills. Now, how many principals or teachers do you think it would take to do your job? You are the person they depend on every day to make the school run smoothly. You are the expert in your department. *You* are the professional.

Characteristics of a Pro

A professional is a person who can do his best at a time when he doesn't particularly feel like it.
— Alistair Cooke

Professionals are responsible. They understand expectations and work toward the goal. They are honest and trustworthy in actions and interactions. Professionals know how to manage their time and demonstrate responsibility in their work.

Professionals seek new knowledge. They learn new and better ways of tackling work. They are not afraid of change, even if they've "always done things that way." Professionals know that the biggest room in the house is the *room for improvement,* and that education is not only for kids. John Wooden says, "It is what you learn after you know it all that really counts."

Professionals dress for success. Professionals know that a neat appearance demonstrates pride in their work. Initial impressions are lasting impressions.

Professionals solve problems on the job. They recognize problems, develop a plan of action, and follow through with the plan. Professionals have the skills to figure out creative solutions rather than blaming others.

Professionals communicate with coworkers and supervisors. They are effective listeners and know how to verbalize their ideas, concerns, and needs. They ask questions to clarify information and to understand situations. Professionals do not react defensively when a coworker disagrees.

Professionals are members of an organization related to their work. For example, I am a member of the National Speakers Association. I attend a convention once a year and learn from industry leaders and fellow speakers. Ask your supervisor to suggest an association related to your trade, and consider general educational organizations that have support staff memberships. Several organizations for school support persons are listed in the Resources section of this book.

Professionals are confident and competent. They believe in their ability and skill in completing the job. They are confident without being arrogant. They do not fear constructive feedback on how to do their job differently because their value and self–worth are internal rather than external.

<u>Professionals are team players.</u> They work with and not against other staff members. The cliché "None of us is as smart as all of us" is a motto close to the hearts of professionals. They understand that every team member is valuable, but that no team member is irreplaceable.

Play for Pay

Amateurs hope. Professionals work.
—*Garson Kanin*

A hobby is an activity you do for fun and relaxation. A profession is an activity you do for pay. Some activities are hobbies for some people and professions for others. Many people like to golf. They pay to play. A professional golfer, however, plays for pay.

Your school principal may be a great chef, but if you are the cafeteria manager or the school cook, then you are the professional. The teachers may have Band–Aids® in the classroom, but the school nurse is the professional. The assistant principal may sign delivery receipts, but the bookkeeper is the professional who follows through with the accounting. The teacher on bus duty may step onto your bus and watch over the children while you run an errand in the building, but you are the professional bus driver. You are the one who sits in the driver's seat. The fifth–grade teacher may be handy with tools, but if you are the custodian, you will be the one called on to fix the broken pencil sharpeners and door hinges. *You are the professional. Your knowledge and ability generate your income.* You see things the non–professional does not see. You have a deeper understanding. There will be times when an administrator or other staff member steps in and performs the first aid in a situation that must be taken care of immediately—similar to the first responders in an accident. If the water cooler is leaking in the hallway, the first responder may know enough to turn off the water valve and unplug the unit, but that only addresses the problem until the professional takes over.

You may not be in the classroom, but the services you provide are just as important to the educational mission of your district as the contributions of teachers and administrators. Whatever your position, your job creates an environment where children are better able to learn. A hungry child cannot learn. A sick child cannot learn. A child without transportation to school cannot learn. A child cannot learn in a building that is dirty and unsafe. A child cannot learn without the support of the educational assistants who provide the extra attention or the secretaries who minimize classroom interruptions.

Now, repeat after me: "I am important to the educational success of children in this school. I am a *professional!*"

Section 2:

Team
Tryouts

CHAPTER THREE

YOURS, MINE, OR OURS?

Individual commitment to a group effort —
that is what makes a team work.
— Vincent Lombardi

Let's face it — we would be nothing without the help of others. Whether at home with our families or on the job with coworkers, we depend on one another to get things done. Teams are groups of people who work together for a common goal. They pull together the strengths and abilities of each member. It is the old "two heads are better than one" approach. Together we are smarter, stronger, and more productive.

If you have children or grandchildren, you know that toddlers do not like to share their toys. As they move through the developmental stages, they learn to interact with other children in play. They engage in side–by–side play where two build with blocks in the same area, often imitating each other, but not working together. Then they learn to play interactively — helping each other build block structures. At this point, they become a simple team, with a common goal of stacking the blocks as high as possible, and they work together to achieve that goal.

In the workplace, you may notice some individuals who do not want to share their "toys," which could be their skills, their knowledge, their tools, or their ideas. They work independently and do not want to be a part of the team. There may be some who work side by side, learning by observing and imitating others, but they still want to work alone. Then there are the team players. Team players are those individuals who recognize how their skills and responsibilities support the overall goal of the school. They understand that every task contributes to the education of the students in the building, and they see themselves as important members of a larger community.

A school has natural teams — teachers, cafeteria workers,

secretaries, custodians, bus drivers, nurses, administrators—and although they may have team–specific goals, they are working toward the overall goal of providing a safe learning experience for students. No matter what your job, every decision you make and every task you complete is ultimately related to the goal of educating the students.

Whose Job Is this Anyway?

It's amazing how much can be accomplished if no one cares who gets the credit.
—Blanton Collier

I love the story about the physician and her husband who were sitting in a fancy restaurant where the service had been anything but fancy. Across the room, one of the waiters grabbed his chest and fell to the ground. Panicked, the host cried out, "Is there a doctor in the room?" The physician identified herself, but then said, "I'm sorry, I can't help—that's not my waiter."

When was the last time you experienced the "it's not my job" level of service? Mine was with my phone company. I was shuffled around more than a deck of cards. I had a simple request that anyone with a pulse could solve, and yet miraculously, it was "not their job." By the way, how do you like giving your life history along with your social security number and mother's maiden name each time your call is transferred?

One well–known auto manufacturer understands this kind of frustration. They've implemented a customer service policy of *one and done*. Their goal is for the first person you speak with to solve your problem or answer your question. If the employee is not able to take care of your concern, he contacts the team member who can help, explains your situation in detail so you do not have to repeat your story, and then transfers the call. This *warm transfer* reflects the fact that the company values your time. Their business is booming!

Likewise, school employees should know enough about their teammates' jobs to step in and help, even when doing so might not be their usual responsibility. Many schools have a receptionist, a secretary, and a bookkeeper in the front office. Their job descriptions are different, but it is essential that they help one another out when the office is busy. If a visitor enters the office and the receptionist is away from the desk, one of the other team members offers to help.

When a call or a request must be transferred, a warm transfer shows the visitor that she is important to the staff. This little extra attention makes the interaction with the school a positive one.

Telice Ostrinski, a secretary in the San Bernardino Unified School District (California), takes every opportunity to learn about the services her team provides to parents and students. Whenever she schedules professional development for school staff, she attends as many as possible so she can better answer questions and serve her customers. The knowledge Telice has gained allows her to field phone calls more efficiently—and provide one–and–done service for the callers, faculty, and on–site visitors.

When Push Comes to Shove

It's not about individual heroes; heroes come in teams.
—John Stanford,
Past Superintendent of Schools, Seattle, WA

HVAC mechanic Richard "Tuck" Tucker says that things go a lot smoother with teamwork. "The fellow I work with, Steve Frush, is very good with air conditioners and I'm good with boilers. If a boiler job comes up, I will take the lead. If it's an air–conditioning job, Steve takes charge." Tuck and his partner are also ready to help the other maintenance workers in the Frederick County Public Schools (Maryland). "When the electricians need help, we jump right in and help pull wires. *When push comes to shove*, we help each other out. That is why things work so well for us."

Cheryl Jalanivich is the superintendent's secretary in Ocean Springs School District (Mississippi). She says, "In the central office, different departments have different seasons of heavy work. I feel teamwork is about supporting one another. It is important to be sensitive to these times of heavier workloads. In my office, we are willing to step in and help in whatever manner we can. We are also responsive to what is going on in a team member's life. Sometimes what a person is enduring at home affects performance in the office, and at times, we need to allow them a little slack and assist however we can."

Head custodian Barry Crocker says, "I am at Nicholson Elementary (Cobb County Schools, Georgia) as a support for the staff and I will do whatever they need—even beyond my custodial duties." In the past, that need has included wearing a cow costume for a fundraiser, dressing as a woman and as a star for school programs, chasing snakes off the playground, changing tires for staff members and parents, and removing a dead possum from under assistant principal Cheryl Mauldin's car!

Barry also accompanies the guidance counselor on home visits to deliver holiday baskets and gifts. He dresses as Santa or an elf for the preschoolers who are at home, so that the delivery appears to come from the North Pole rather than charity from the school. "I get to go into the homes," Barry says, "and then in January the kids are showing me the new coat they got for Christmas, or telling me about the goodies they received. You walk away, knowing that for that one moment you have helped a child."

Another way Barry provides Sizzling Service is by being *a partner, not a pointer*. He is often asked directions when visitors see him working on the school grounds. Instead of pointing the way, Barry walks them inside and introduces them to the office staff. It only takes Barry a few minutes to offer this customer courtesy, and it leaves a lasting impression.

Less Me, More We

Talent wins games, but teamwork wins championships.
— *Michael Jordan*

Team players realize that others depend on them to complete their own tasks. A team performs like a machine: if one gear is disengaged, the rest of the machine cannot work properly. For instance, the custodians depend on the clinic assistant to properly dispose of hazardous waste so the cleaning staff is not at risk. The cafeteria workers depend on the teachers to prepare an accurate lunch count each morning so they can cook enough food for students, staff, and visitors. The secretaries depend on the teachers to send correct attendance reports to the office so they can get the information logged into the computer for the district. The bus drivers depend on the office staff to process bus passes for new students so they can deliver children to the correct address. The teachers depend on the bus drivers to get the students to school safely and on time.

Perhaps the school nurse does not complete the vision and hearing screenings within the state–mandated timelines. This affects the school secretary, who is not able to complete the health cards in the cumulative folders before the state records audit.

What if the lead custodian forgets to order soap and paper towels? If the other custodians do not have the supplies to restock the classrooms, the students will not be able to clean their hands, which could lead to spreading of germs. And on it goes.

Every responsibility left unattended has an effect on others. Who is inconvenienced (or worse) when we do not hold up our end of the team responsibility?

Moving the Team Forward

The real secret of success is enthusiasm.
   —*Walter Chrysler*

Our attitude determines whether we help move the team forward or drag it down. I would rather work with an enthusiastic team member than a complainer who loves to find the negative side of things. Now, do not think that a person must be Mr. Always Bubbly or Ms. Stand–up Comedienne to have enthusiasm. Enthusiasm comes from a positive attitude and can bolster team spirit even in the midst of difficulties.

Let's compare two school nurses with identical training and credentials. Both have the same experience. Both wear those popular scrub outfits with the cool designs that the students like. One nurse has enthusiasm for her work. She loves the students and enjoys being around her coworkers. The other nurse works only for her salary. She is quick to diagnose a student's stomach ache as merely an excuse to get out of class, and she makes derogatory comments about the teachers sending so many children to the clinic. Who do you think is going to be the best team member and provide the best customer service for the students: Nurse Sunshine or Nurse Shadow?

Joanne Jones is a Nurse Sunshine. She is attentive to the needs of the whole child—including physical, emotional, and social needs. She dispenses medications *and* tender loving care in the clinic at Woestina Elementary School (Schalmont Central School District, New York). If a child is sick and needs to go home, she arranges for that to happen. Sometimes, though, a little encouragement and a listening ear are all that a child needs to go back in the classroom.

Joanne worked with the Parent Teacher Organization to

implement a walking club and serves on the Heath Advisory Committee. She also volunteers to be a surrogate parent for students on field trips and other school activities that require parental involvement. Joanne wants students to have a positive experience when they come to the clinic and return to the classroom ready to learn.

John Dorman, custodian at Griffin Elementary School (Broward County Public Schools, Florida) understands how embarrassed students feel when they vomit on the floor. Often students are apologetic when John comes to clean up the mess, but he assures them that it is no big deal, that it could happen to anybody, and that he does not mind taking care of the situation. His good–natured approach helps to preserve dignity during a stressful time for the student. He maintains his enthusiasm even when the job is not pleasant.

Gelotology and the Workplace (Yes, It's Legal)

Laughter is the closest distance between two people.
— Victor Borge

Nothing holds a team together like laughter. And laughter can improve your health as well! Why, there is even a field of science — gelotology — devoted to the study of laughter and the physiological and psychological effects it has on the body. (No, the root word for gelotology is not the same as the root word for Jell–O®, even though Jell–O® appears to be laughing when it jiggles.) These studies show that laughing reduces stress and anxiety, lowers blood sugar levels, increases pain tolerance, and strengthens the immune system. The physical act of laughing also contributes to overall physical fitness. A hearty laugh exercises the facial, respiratory, abdominal, diaphragm, back, and leg muscles.

In his book *Primal Leadership,* Daniel Goleman points out that laughter is one emotion that easily spreads from one person to another. When you hear others laughing, you laugh in response — even if you do not know why they are laughing. When you see others crying, you may try to comfort them, but you do not automatically start crying. Goleman says, "In any work setting, therefore, the sound of laughter signals the group's emotional temperature."

Marcia Forsythe is a kindergarten assistant and a lunchroom monitor at Kemptown Elementary School (Frederick County Public Schools, Maryland). She understands the importance of laughter at work. Her principal, Steve Parsons, says that Marcia always has a smile for those around her. Assistant principal Catherine Poling says that Marcia is the only person she has danced with in the hallways! It seems they nearly knocked each other over coming through a door one day, so to the delight of the students standing nearby, Marcia took Catherine's hands and led her in a grand waltz!

In the classroom and in the lunchroom, Marcia continues to bring smiles to staff and students. At the end of the lunch period, Marcia leads a "Joke Time" with the students. She says, "They are dying to tell these jokes—sometimes they forget the punch–line, or the jokes don't make sense, but it's a good end of the cafeteria time." Sense or nonsense, everyone loves the silliness of a joke. Marcia probably knows more "knock–knocks" than anyone else in her building! Fond memories spring from the little things we do for children, and every time students see Marcia, whether at school or in the community, they will associate her with happy times.

You do not have to socialize outside of work to have fun with your team members. Help one another. Give a birthday card. Bring brownies to work and share them. Learn to laugh with your coworkers and laugh a lot! Laughter adds years to your life and life to your years. So take joy in your job. Laughter and joy are contagious and can enhance the cohesiveness of your team.

Everybody Is Normal until You Get to Know Them

Nothing is so simple that it cannot be misunderstood.
—Jr. Teague

Even if team members are supportive and enthusiastic and enjoy working together, there will be misunderstandings and friction from time to time. As someone once said, "Everybody is normal until you get to know them." Experts on teaming agree that every high–performing team will go through a "storming" phase. Do not panic. Keep the communication lines open. If you are unsure about something, check it out. Talk to your teammates, listen to their suggestions, offer your thoughts, and be willing to compromise. Misunderstandings clear up when teammates communicate with one another.

Rules for the Road

Rules are for the obedience of fools and the guidance of wise men.
—*Douglas Bader*

One way to make sure you and your team members are on the same page regarding expectations and commitments is to develop *principles of operation for your team* at the beginning of the school year. This is a magical communication tool that solves problems before they happen. As a team leader, I do this by asking members to describe teams they have served on that were *not* effective. I write out their comments on flip–chart paper or a white board. Since all of us have been on ineffective teams, I get a long list in a short period. The list usually goes something like this:

1. One person dominated team meetings.
2. We did not start or end on time.
3. Team members gossipped about other team members.
4. All talk and no action.
5. Unclear goals.
6. Personality conflicts.
7. Certain team members did not pull their weight.

I turn all these negatives into positives. For example, no one will speak twice until everyone has had a chance to speak. Then I ask every team member to make these our *rules for the road*. Once we have adopted our rules, we post them in a prominent place and hold one another accountable to follow them.

Assessing Your Teaming IQ

Snowflakes are one of nature's most fragile things, but just look at what they can do when they stick together.
—*Vesta Kelly*

A team player realizes not only how important his or her job is, but also the importance of others' jobs. Team players are interdependent rather than independent. How do you measure up on these team domains?

1. **Engaged Team Members Stand Together**
   Do I work well with others?
   Do I help my teammates, even when the job is not mine?
   Do I applaud the successes of others or hog the glory?
   Do I support or divide?

2. **Engaged Team Members Communicate Effectively**
   Do I ask questions when I do not understand something?
   Do I listen to the concerns of my teammates?
   Do I share my concerns in a positive manner?

3. **Engaged Team Members Embrace Change**
   Do I give new ideas a chance or dig in my heels and refuse to consider them?
   Do I handle interruptions to my schedule with flexibility or frustration?
   When faced with change, do I ask why, or why not?

4. **Engaged Team Members Have a Positive Spirit**
   Am I an encourager or a grumbler?
   Do I have a good attitude or a *bad–itude*?
   Do I believe serving others is a noble profession?
   Do I see setbacks as permanent or temporary?

5. **Engaged Team Members Find Fun in the Workplace**
   Do I enjoy being with my teammates?
   Do I find pleasure in my job?
   Do others see my enthusiasm?
   Do I bring a sense of humor to the workplace?

Engaged Ambassadors Are Effective Team Members

When you are a supportive and positive team member, you become a more engaged ambassador for your school. Your interactions with coworkers, students, parents, and the community reflect your positive attitude and pride in being a part of the educational team.

Disengaged Employees	Engaged Ambassadors
☒ Prefer working alone	☑ Support and depend on the team
☒ Seek self–glory	☑ Are enthusiastic
☒ Display a negative attitude	☑ Bring joy to the job
☒ Are jealous of others	☑ Applaud teammates' success
☒ Focus on individual tasks	☑ Share time, skills, and encouragement to create team success
	☑ Communicate with clarity

CHAPTER FOUR

DIFFERENT PEOPLE, DIFFERENT PERSONALITIES

*Our greatest strength as a human race is to acknowledge our differences,
our greatest weakness is our failure to embrace them.*
— Judith Henderson

Just as team members have different knowledge, skills, and job descriptions, they also have different personalities. When we understand the basic personality types, we better understand our team members and can use that understanding to increase our team success.

The DiSC is a Personal Profile System that looks at behavioral patterns and translates them into four main dimensions: dominance, influence, steadiness, and conscientiousness. When I teach how to build Turbo Teams, I administer the DiSC assessment (DiSC® Classic Personal Profile System 2800, Inscape Publishing) and help team members understand that most colleagues are not difficult…they are just different. We laugh and learn as I describe the four types of people you and I interact with on a daily basis.

The Four Types

1. Dominant Directors (Dominance Personality): Their motto is *lead, follow, or get out of the way.*

Team members with a Dominance Personality are decision makers who are not afraid to take action to overcome opposition and achieve their goals.

Dominant Directors:
- tackle decision–making and unpleasant situations directly
- are focused
- deal with change, welcoming it as a contest to be won.

All strengths have corresponding limitations, evidence that we need one another. In their quest to get the job done, Dominant Directors may seem impatient to move before the team is ready. If you are a Dominant Director, you have probably been told more than once that you would be more effective by slowing down and listening more. I know what you are thinking. *It is not that I do not listen. Other people do not speak up. Why can't my team members be more assertive like me and say what is really on their minds?* Opposites do attract—but then they tend to attack. The key is to stay humble. Celebrate your strengths while accepting and appreciating how your other team members are "wired."

2. Interacting Socializers (Influence Personality): Their motto is *it does not matter whether you win or lose, but how you look when you play the game.*

Team members with this personality type are "persuaders" rather than "tellers." They use their influence to move the team toward the goals.

Interacting Socializers:
- are enthusiastic and inspirational
- have a positive attitude and see the positive in others
- are generous with their time for teammates.

Interacting Socializers are often overly optimistic about the effort it will take to accomplish a task. We love them because of their positive spirit and enthusiasm, a trait which, if overused, can spread them too thin and give the appearance of disorganization. Team members who resist change frustrate Interacting Socializers. They want everyone to be as excited about the future as they are. If you are an Interacting Socializer, it is important to remember that many times these "negative" individuals are not intentionally trying to rain on your parade. They simply see all the things that might go wrong as clearly as you see the silver lining in every dark cloud.

As an Interacting Socializer, I have learned to accept and appreciate what the more systematic, methodical types bring to the table. I am not as effective without them. I see these types as realists who balance out my optimism, rather than naysayers attempting to throw wet blankets on my brilliant ideas.

3. Steady Relaters (Steadiness Personality): Their motto is *why can't we all just get along*?

Team members with a Steadiness Personality like to keep things on an even keel. They are peacemakers. They prefer to work toward team goals using the resources already available and proven.

Steady Relaters:
- are more interested in making their surroundings better than radically changing their environment
- are cooperative, patient, and loyal
- are good listeners, but may not be assertive in their own communication.

In their quest to get the job done, Steady Relaters may avoid conflict and change, and can be indecisive. They usually work best within established routines.

One of my daughters is a Steady Relater. She is easygoing, cooperative, and the most sensitive of all my five children. When we have family debates on where to go for dinner or vacation, she is the last one to speak up and her response is typically, "It doesn't matter to me. Where do the others want to go?" Steady Relaters are the ones you ask to pick you up at the airport at midnight. (Dominant Directors would be glad to pick you up, but you are afraid to ask them!)

If you are a Steady Relater, let me encourage you not to be afraid of occasional conflict. Whenever you rub shoulders with people, you are going to knock a few heads. Your ideas are important and the team suffers when you do not jump in with your thoughts, even if they are contrary to what the team is currently thinking.

4. Cautious Thinkers (Conscientiousness Personality): Their motto is *not whether you win or lose, but how you play the game.*

Team members with a Conscientiousness Personality are systematic and analytical in their approach towards team goals.

Cautious Thinkers:
- value accuracy and diplomacy
- pay attention to details
- deal with conflict indirectly.

In their quest to get the job done, Cautious Thinkers want all details to be perfect. They may appear unfriendly due to their focus on details. These team members place a high value on following the rules.

One of my best friends has the behavioral tendencies of a Cautious Thinker. He is fun to observe because he is so different from me. When he gets a new vehicle, he runs out of gas on purpose just to see exactly how many miles per gallon his vehicle gets. Okay, that was just a little dig at my friend. He is not that obsessive. It is, however, amazing to watch him work. He is meticulous, and thorough, and has high standards. His work area is neat as a pin before he leaves every day, while my desk more often than not looks like a pigpen.

If you are a Cautious Thinker, here is a tip on how to be a more effective team member: *Loosen up a little.* Inside, you are a creative, engaging person. The problem is that often only your closest friends know this about you. In the workplace, you can come across as aloof and rigid because of your attention to the task. You sometimes overreact if things do not go as you have planned or if others do not seem to appreciate your effort to do things right. Rest assured that although they do not always express it, the other personality styles appreciate the fact that you worry about all those important things that they neglect. Cautious Thinkers and Steady Relaters are the glue that holds organizations together.

Complementary Differences

We don't accomplish anything in this world alone...and whatever happens is the result of the whole tapestry of one's life and all the weavings of individual threads from one to another that creates something.
— Sandra Day O'Connor

Writing this book has been a team effort. I have been researching and speaking on Sizzling Customer Service for years. It is easier for me to talk about Customer Service than it is for me to write about it. I am an Interacting Socializer. I get my energy from being around people and love interruptions around the office. If we do not have any, I create them. Vie, on the other hand, is a Steady Relater with Conscientious as a secondary dimension. She is easy going and warm toward others, but is much more structured than I am. Together, we were able to fulfill our dream of writing a book to honor and encourage support staff.

Engaged Ambassadors Seek to Understand Differences

Now, do not go hanging out your therapist shingle and trying to analyze everything your team members say or do. Instead, use this information as intended: to give you a general understanding of how different personality types can work together. Engaged ambassadors embrace differences and channel them to increase team success.

Disengaged Employees	Engaged Ambassadors
☒ Weaken the team by magnifying differences	☑ Embrace differences to strengthen the team
☒ Are threatened by differences	☑ Appreciate different perspectives
☒ See no way but their way	☑ Invite differing approaches to view problems/solutions from all sides

Section 3:

Communication

CHAPTER FIVE

YOU THOUGHT I SAID WHAT?

The problem with communication...
is the illusion that it has been accomplished.
—*George Bernard Shaw*

Communication is the sharing or exchange of information between two or more people, and includes both verbal and nonverbal components. Communication takes place in a loop—referred to as "the communication model." Here is how it works:

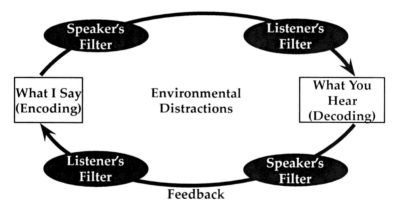

- What I mean, filtered through my personal experience and knowledge, is translated into what I say. This is called encoding.
- What I say travels through the air as sound waves and stimulates the hearing mechanism of my listener.
- What my listener hears is translated into what my listener understands, filtered through personal experience and knowledge as well as any distractions in the environment. This is called decoding, and influences my listener's feedback to me.

Can you see any possibility of miscommunication? Perhaps what you intended, and thought was perfectly clear is not how the listener interpreted what he heard. Perhaps you were speaking in a noisy environment and the listener missed part of what you said. Perhaps your experiences and knowledge are different from that of the listener. Many times, I know exactly what I am trying to communicate in my head but struggle to find the right words so that it makes sense to the listener. Can you relate? The communication circuit is never complete without feedback to ensure that both parties understand each other.

Here is an example of a bus driver using the feedback loop to clarify information from the principal:

"Mary, are you available to drive the third period Spanish class to the Peruvian embassy for their tour next Wednesday?"

Instead of just replying yes, the bus driver gets clarification by asking questions. This exchange of information completes the feedback loop:

"Yes. What time should I be here?"
"No later than eight AM. You'll take care of all the details, won't you?"
"What details do you mean?"
"You'll have the voucher for the toll road and the pass for DC parking, right?"
"No. When you send the field–trip request to transportation, they will include those items with your confirmation."
"Request? I forgot to tell the new teacher she needed to send that form to transportation. Thanks for reminding me."

Communication Strategies that Work in the Trenches

You can have brilliant ideas, but if you can't get them across, your ideas won't get you anywhere.
                                                    —Lee Iacocca

I frequently get frantic calls from couples in marital trouble or from corporations where the board room has turned into a war room. Communication has broken down and the caller is looking for a mediator to get some people talking and other people listening. More often than not, I have been able to turn these explosive situations into productive sessions where effective two–way communication once again flows freely. The following strategies have helped others, and they can help you too.

- **Be sincere in your communication with others.**
  Show your sincerity by making eye contact with the recipient and making sure he or she has acknowledged you before speaking. Align your tone of voice, your body language, and your words.
- **Increase clarity 100 percent by asking questions.**
  Ask clarifying questions to be sure that you are understood, and to filter what you have heard. One of my favorite techniques is to restate what someone has just told me, and then to ask this simple open–ended question: "What have I missed?"
- **Know the purpose of your communication.**
  Is it to gather or share information? Is it to be social? Perhaps you want to encourage others or enlist their help, or your purpose may be to seek a change in behavior. A focused purpose leads to productive conversation. Have you heard of *mixed messages*? This is what happens when a conversation tries to accomplish too many things. How do you feel when someone says that you are doing a good job, then adds the word *but*? Do you feel set up? Try this instead: "I would like to speak with you about (be specific). When is a good time for us to talk?" I have learned that just because it is a good time for me does not mean it is a good time for the recipient.
- **Use vocal variety to make it easy for others to listen to you.**
  Have you ever been in a meeting where the speaker was very knowledgeable about the subject but spoke in a monotone? Your attention wanders and you might even catch some ZZZZZ's. (I know why people take sunglasses to seminars.) Communication is a two–way street, and the speaker can help the listener to attend. This is true whether you are speaking to a group or an individual. The number–one technique for holding a listener's attention is to use variety in your rate of speech, your pitch, and your volume. In addition to these aspects of voice, I also use pauses or lengthen words for emphasis. For example, if I am speaking to a large group, and I notice that the after–lunch sluggishness is setting in, I might pause for a moment. The silence invariably results in the

audience turning to look in my direction. Sometimes the group will get noisy while I am speaking. I could raise my voice over the chatter, but it is more effective if I switch to a soft voice. And if I want to make a special point, I might lengthen a word for emphasis. Vocal variety reels your audience in and helps them to be better listeners. It is as if you have a sign on your chest: "You may not like me, but you cannot ignore me."

- **Draw others into the conversation.**
  You can do this by asking people for their opinions and encouraging their contributions by nodding or agreeing with their comments. When you respect the comments of others, they will be more willing to engage in discussion with you.
- **Be careful not to interrupt the speaker.**
  Concentrate on what the speaker is saying and save your comments until he or she has finished talking. This might require a few teeth marks on the tongue, but it's worth it.

The Don CeSar Method for Classy Communication

The basic building block of good communication is the feeling that every human being is unique and of value.
—Unknown

If you have ever been to St. Petersburg, Florida, you have probably seen the Don CeSar Hotel. Built in 1928, this historic pink "castle" has been a point of reference on maritime navigation maps for many years. The Don CeSar is one classy place. The rooms have super–thick towels and there are two luxurious terry robes in every closet. A sign on the hanger says, "These robes are here for your comfort. These robes may be purchased in the Don Cesar shop." Now, what they are really saying is, "Don't steal the robes." However, the Don CeSar says this in a classy way that is not offensive.

In my travels, I have also stayed at Motel Stix—you know, the one that does not leave the light on for you. They also have a sign in their rooms. It is usually a black sign with white letters or a white sign with black letters and it says, "An inventory has been taken of this room. If any items are missing, your credit card will be charged." I get irritated when I read that sign. Although they do not know me, it is almost as if they are accusing me of being a thief.

Now, both of these businesses are communicating that the

guest room items are not to be taken, but which way is the most effective? How do you think guests react to the sign in the Don CeSar? How about the Motel Stix?

The Don CeSar is a classy place, and it communicates in a classy manner. The Don CeSar does not point a finger. The guest's dignity is respected and protected. The Motel Stix method is accusatory and assumes the worst of its guests. In comparison to the Don CeSar's classy style, the Motel Stix has a tacky style. Would you rather be a classy or a tacky communicator?

Think about how you handle potentially stressful or crucial conversations. Are you able to communicate your needs in a positive manner that preserves the dignity of your listener? Let the Don CeSar method be your point of reference when navigating the waters of crucial communication.

The Four–step way to navigate using the Don CeSar method:

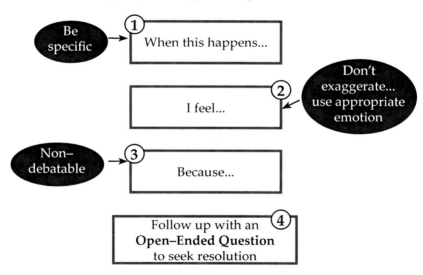

Okay, let's fill in those blanks. Suppose the custodian keeps his tools and equipment in the workroom. The teachers on the fifth–grade team often borrow the stepladder. That would be fine, except they forget to return it promptly, if at all. The custodian could handle this situation by going to the principal and reporting the team, or he could approach the teachers and maturely express his concerns using the Don CeSar method:

- **When this happens:** "When my equipment is missing from the workroom..."
- **Feeling statement:** "I become concerned."
- **Because statement:** "A student might climb the ladder and be injured. And I can't change the fluorescent tubes in the office until I track down the ladder."
- **Seek resolution:** "What can we do to make sure that my equipment is returned before the students arrive?"

Look at the "when this happens" statement. The custodian did not say, "When *you* take my equipment." Rather, he calmly described the situation without putting blame on anyone.

The custodian then took responsibility for his own feelings and needs by using an "I–message." He stated, "I feel concerned," rather than "You made me concerned." This avoids putting the listener on the defensive and leads into the "because" statement.

"Because" statements must be non–debatable. A student can be injured on a ladder. That is non–debatable. The custodian needs his ladder to change the light tubes. That is also non–debatable.

The last step seeks resolution by asking an open–ended question. There is no finger pointing, but the responsibility shifts back to the listener. It also shows that the speaker is willing to assist in a solution.

When you use the Don CeSar method, you are able to calmly discuss the situation and work toward a resolution. Accurately verbalizing your feelings is the tricky part. When you are upset, your vocabulary may become limited. Words like *frustrated*, *angry*, or *furious* might be the first that pop into your mind. It is important to choose the right emotional word to match the situation.

The first time the custodian approaches the teachers, the words *anxious* or *concerned* would be the better way to describe his feelings. If the situation continues to happen, the next conversation might use a stronger emotion. Perhaps he would say, "I feel disappointed because we had worked out a plan where the ladder would be returned before the students arrived." If the problem still occurs, the feeling word might escalate to *frustrated*.

It is often embarrassing when we *react* rather than *respond* to stressful encounters. Take a few minutes to cool down and consider this scenario:

A supervisor is speaking to one of the secretaries:

"You were rolling your eyes during the entire staff training seminar. I am angry because you were being disrespectful to the speaker. What do you have to say for yourself?"

Now look at the secretary's response:

"I am sorry you feel that way, but I was not being disrespectful. I recently started wearing contact lenses and they were irritating my eyes. I did not want to miss any of the information by leaving the room."

The supervisor now feels foolish for assuming he knew why the secretary was rolling her eyes. The only way to know for sure why a person has acted a certain way is to ask—and then listen to the answer. By approaching critical conversations calmly, and not jumping to conclusions, you will avoid many miscommunications. Dr. Stephen Covey reminds us to "Seek first to understand, and then to be understood."

Nonverbal Communication

The most important thing in communication is hearing what isn't said.
— Peter Drucker

What you do not say is often more important than what you share verbally. Nonverbal communication accounts for 50 to 95 percent of the actual communication. Have you ever seen a child required to apologize when she is really not sorry? Her "I'm sorry" may be accompanied by a scowl, folded arms, and an angry tone. Her body language speaks louder than her words.

Here are the major components of nonverbal communication, or body language:

- Facial expressions
- Posture and spatial position of the body
- Gestures of the hands

- Movements of the arms, shoulders, or head
- Eye contact
- Silence
- Voice tone

You may have had a conversation with someone whose body language did not match his or her verbal communication. When that happens, you can usually be sure that what they don't say is the real message they would like to be sending.

Effective communicators use nonverbal cues to strengthen what they say. For instance, your body language should support your words. People want to know that your communication is honest. Your sincerity must show in your verbal and your nonverbal communication.

Listening for Intent, Not Just Content

God gave man two ears but only one mouth that he might hear twice as much as he speaks.
—*Greek Philosopher Epictetus*

Excellent listeners are onto something so good that I call it the "Enchantment of Effective Listening." Being a good listener endears you to others. People will become loyal to you and committed to you and go the extra mile, because they know you care. When you are a good listener, you make the speaker feel valued and accepted.

Sherry Cunningham is a bus driver and special education assistant at Unity School in the Lincoln County School System (Tennessee). Sherry knows the importance of listening to the students on her bus—listening to what they say as well as what they do not say. Sherry says, "The bus driver needs to pick up on the emotions of a child. It is important to ask if you can do anything for the child—and then listen. Children will know if you are not sincere. They need to know that the adults in their world care about them. By being a good listener, you let them know you love and respect them."

Bus driver Jim Murley (Waxahachie Independent School District, Texas) agrees with Sherry. He says, "The big thing I've found out with kids is that they want to be listened to. They do not want you to say, 'Yeah, yeah', and not really hear them. There is a difference between hearing and listening."

Jim is right; hearing is not the same as listening. Good listeners:

- Listen with their eyes, ears, and heart to understand the real message
- Listen for the intent as well as the content
- Pay attention and ignore distractions
- Engage in only one conversation at a time
- Maintain good eye contact
- Use posture and body language to convey interest in what is being said
- Don't interrupt or change the subject
- Clarify the speaker's intent by asking questions
- Give the speaker thinking time—don't jump in to supply words when the speaker is gathering her thoughts
- Treat conversations with dignity and confidentiality, and do not gossip

Being an effective listener is hard work and it takes practice. We listen at a rate of 600 words per minute, while spoken communication occurs at only 150 words per minute (with gusts up to 300 wpm when we are angry). Because we listen (or think) faster than the spoken word, it takes a conscious effort to pay attention to what is being said and not think ahead to what we are going to say next. I often give "all day" seminars. I am literally on my feet and running my mouth for six hours. I used to feel sorry for myself, and truthfully, I would whine a little at the end of the day about the amount of energy I expended and how hard I worked to engage participants. I do not do that anymore. Now I end my seminars by giving a standing ovation to the listeners. They were the ones who, if they truly focused on our topic, worked the hardest.

Calvin Coolidge said, "No one ever listened him or herself out of a job." Sometimes when we are quick to speak, we end up with a foot in the mouth. Listeners do not have that problem, do they?

Engaged Ambassadors Are Effective Communicators

Whenever you talk to friends or neighbors about your job, you have the opportunity to share positive comments about your place of work. Use your communication skills to build up your coworkers, your supervisors, your school, and the school district. Your words can change attitudes and clear up misconceptions.

Disengaged Employees	Engaged Ambassadors
☒ Speak without concern for others' feelings	☑ Value the input of others
☒ Are more concerned with formulating their next comment than with listening to others	☑ Encourage others to contribute to the conversation
☒ Expect others to read their minds	☑ Build others up with their words
☒ Assume understanding on the part of the listener	☑ Check for understanding in a conversation
☒ Relay one message with their words and a different message with their body language	☑ Listen when others are speaking
	☑ Look to nonverbal cues for better understanding

CHAPTER SIX

STICKS AND STONES

Kind words can be short and easy to speak,
but their echoes are truly endless.
—Mother Teresa

Many adults forget how powerful their words are to the young people around them. Since children do not usually give us immediate feedback, it is easy to assume that what we say does not matter. Few people (children and adults alike) come back and say, "What you said meant a lot to me," or, "When I was at school you were so encouraging and you always had a smile on your face," or, "You always said something nice to me."

Because we do not always get that feedback, we make the erroneous assumption that our words and behaviors are not affecting the lives of kids. Sometimes I remind audiences about a classic story in the Bible where ten lepers were healed and only one came back to say thanks. Your positive words and encouraging actions have an influence, whether you ever hear the words "thank you" or not. Children and young people may not realize the impact you have had on their lives until they are grown.

If more people were coming back and thanking us, we would say, "Wow! This is powerful; I'm going to do it more." You are positively affecting others whether they acknowledge it or not. You may recall an adult who encouraged you in school—it is never too late to pick up the phone or send them a letter of thanks. Hearing from you will make their day!

At the same time, you may have memories of unkind words— proof that the words of others leave indelible marks on our spirits.

Teaching assistant Pauline Cowan was timid when she was a youngster. "I was taller than the other girls and they teased me," she recalls. Her mother comforted her and said, "God made this earth big enough for all of us."

Pauline says, "My mom told me to use what I had. I am thankful for a mom who encouraged me and gave me confidence when I was a child." Pauline's mother helped her to believe in herself—and she ended up becoming a teen fashion model. As an adult, Pauline was widowed with three small children. Her faith and her positive self–esteem were essential to her success in directing a child–care facility for a large corporation while being a single parent.

Pauline's children are grown now and she retired from directing the child–care center. She did not stay retired very long, though. Her love of children led to her current employment as an assistant teacher for preschoolers at South Knox Elementary (Tennessee). Pauline says, "If I can build self–confidence in a child, I know I'm making a lasting impact. Children are like a bouquet of flowers—each one is unique and special."

Melody Sankey, secretary at Newcastle Middle School (Weston County School District, Wyoming), points out that a kind word and showing that you care is important to older students as well. She says, "Middle–school students still need TLC. These kids are trying to figure out where they belong in life. They are realizing that they are not little kids anymore, but not adults yet. I try to make them feel good about themselves. I faced many of the same things they are facing when I was in middle school. I feel like I can relate to them much better because of that."

Bus driver Stephanie Townsend transports preschool, elementary, middle, and high–school students for Amelia County Public Schools (Virginia). She feels that the high–school students on her bus need as much encouragement as the younger ones. "I'm the first school person the kids see in the mornings. I think I play an important part in whether they have a good day or not. I talk to them. I tell them good morning. When they get off the bus, I tell them to have a great day. I want them to start their day happy."

On their birthdays, Stephanie gives her riders a miniature birthday cake. She says, "Sometimes the high–school students feel like they are shoved to the back. They appreciate that someone has taken the time to give them something special and wish them a happy birthday." Who knows? Those little cakes may be the only celebration some of her students have.

Stephanie says, "I have a great bus. I am proud of my kids and I tell them that. You know, when you are growing up, you want somebody to say that they are proud of you."

My oldest daughter, Bethany, is a senior at Virginia Tech. Whenever I ask her how she is doing, she replies in a deep and funny voice, "Just trying to make you proud, Dad." I suspect that beneath that humor is the desire of all children—to make a significant adult in their life proud.

That Was a Compliment?

What do we live for, if it is not to make it less difficult for each other?
— *George Eliot*

I overheard this conversation between two adults:

"Some kids don't know a compliment when they hear one."

"You're right about that! Yesterday Bob helped me with a chore and I told him thanks for helping me without having his usual attitude. He just stared at me as if he didn't have a clue what I was talking about. I've told him a hundred times to lose the attitude. I finally waved my hand in his face and said, 'Earth to Bob, wake up. Just say thank you for the compliment.'"

Do you hear a twinge of sarcasm in the words spoken to Bob? Does it sound like the speaker really respects this student? Do you think this compliment will decrease the chances of Bob having an "attitude" in the future?

Engaged Ambassadors are encouragers, and encouragers accentuate the positive. It is one of those inverse formulas in life. If you want to decrease a negative behavior, encourage the desired behavior by drawing attention to it. Let's look at a different way to have this same conversation with Bob:

"Bob, thank you for helping me pick up the supplies and put them away. I like how neat the work area looks now, and your smile and willingness to help me has brightened my whole day. Thank you!"

In this second example, the speaker told Bob exactly what she liked: he picked up the supplies, put them away, had a smile, and was willing to help. It does not matter that in the past Bob had an attitude.

Today, he was a smiling and willing helper. A sincere compliment will encourage Bob to repeat the positive behaviors and will help improve his self–esteem.

In her book *Tongue Fu! At School*, Sam Horn says that we need to lose the words *don't, won't, stop,* and *not* if we want to change a behavior. She says, "As long as we keep (these words) in our communication with what we don't want, we'll keep getting what we don't want. If we start communicating what we *do* want, we'll get more of that."

She goes on to say, "You focus on what they should not do, so they continue to cause trouble....You say what you'd like them to do, so they act in accordance with your trust."

Engaged Ambassadors Are Encouragers

Our words and kindnesses can encourage positive self–esteem in students. The words we speak today may be the words that give them hope and the foundation for a positive and productive adulthood. Whether you are the superintendent or the cafeteria worker, your words and actions on the job and in the community reflect on the school and *influence the future of children*. Communicate with kindness!

Disengaged Employees	Engaged Ambassadors
☒ Treat students with disrespect	☑ Understand the power of the spoken word
☒ Do not consider the feelings of students	☑ Desire to nurture positive self–esteem in students
☒ Think words are harmless	☑ Use their words to build up, never to tear down
☒ Use sarcasm in their communications	☑ Encourage others with their words
☒ Are insincere with their encouragement	

Section 4:

Conflict, Anger, and Change

CHAPTER SEVEN

HOW TO SAY WHAT YOU MEAN WITHOUT SAYING IT MEAN

> Conflict is the price we have to pay
> for deeper relationships.
> —Dr. David Seamands

My friend Jim Hebel has seen me at my best and at my worst. We sometimes fight like brothers, but over the years, we have managed to work through our differences and disappointments in constructive ways. We forged a rare friendship in today's world of superficiality. The key to our relationship is trust. We now know (after setting off some landmines over the years) that any anger or conflict must be directed toward the issue and not the person. We learned to say what we mean, mean what we say, but not say it in a mean way. We learned to ask for forgiveness when we were arrogant or had taken our friendship for granted.

Dr. Kenneth Blanchard, one of the best–selling authors of all time, wrote in *We Are the Beloved* that most of us live in two acts. Act I is to achieve, make a name for ourselves, and be successful. Act II is to connect relationally with others. As we become wiser, we realize that people are more important than things. When we are unable or unwilling to work through conflict, we sacrifice relationships with those around us.

Conflict occurs when there is a disagreement, a struggle, or a clash of ideas. But constructive conflict is merely a search for truth. Conflicts can occur over trivial or important matters in the school. In *Crucial Conversations: Tools for Talking When the Stakes Are High,* the authors remind us that in every controversy, each person has his or her "story." Resolution is more likely when we acknowledge and seek to understand the other person's story rather than trying to prove that ours is the only story that matters. High–performing teams see conflict as a chance to grow. They accept and appreciate differences of opinion and are not afraid to have crucial conversations in their efforts to move the school forward.

Five Options for Handling Conflict Situations

Whenever you're in conflict with someone, there is one factor that can make the difference between damaging your relationship and deepening it. That factor is attitude.
—*William James*

When faced with conflict, people usually react by withdrawing, smoothing over the issue, compromising, taking control, or partnering to seek resolution. Let's take a look at each of these options.

1. **Withdraw from the Situation**
    The withdrawer avoids conflict by walking away. One man and woman who were married fifty years illustrate this approach. At their golden–anniversary celebration, someone asked the man, "What's the secret to your marital success?"
    "Well," drawled the man, "my wife and I had an agreement when we got married. If she was bothered about something she would tell me off, get it out of her system. When I got upset, I was supposed to take a walk. I guess you could attribute our marital success to the fact that I have largely led an outdoor life."
    We chuckle at this little story because many of us are just like this husband. Whenever there is a conflict, we "take a walk," or withdraw. Although this approach is not healthy if it becomes a pattern, there are times when withdrawing is the best choice. When you are in a lose/lose situation, walk away. If a conflict is escalating to the point that you or others around you may be in danger, withdraw and get help.
2. **Smooth Over the Situation**
    The smoother gives in rather than dealing with conflict. She wants to please everyone. She says, "I'll lose to please. This issue is not that important to me." As much as I hate to admit this to my readers, this is my preferred style. I grew up in a home where my dad ruled with an iron fist. As mentioned earlier, he was a truck driver and often arrived home short on sleep and with a short fuse. When he got mad, I learned to placate. Whatever it took to calm the storm and keep the peace.
    I will never forget my first job after college. After two weeks

on the job, I had a conflict with my boss. I scheduled a meeting to manage this conflict constructively, but during the meeting, I shriveled up like a prune and never even brought up the situation that was bothering me. I was so mad at myself.

The lessons we learn about dealing with conflict from our family of origin stay with us for a long time. Most adults handle conflict the way it was modeled growing up, and for many of us, these are not healthy patterns.

3. **Seek Compromise with the Situation**

The compromiser will make concessions, but seeks fairness in the resolution. She says, "I will meet you halfway. You give a little. I will give a little." The problem with compromise, if not used in the right situation, is that instead of both parties winning, both parties lose. Many people compromise too quickly in order to avoid the stress of disagreement. The next time you are tempted to compromise, communicate a little bit longer and see if you can discover a point of view that is superior to the position that is causing all the fuss.

4. **Control the Situation**

The controller is determined to get his way. He is often competitive and sees his goals as more important than other goals that are on the table. The controller says, "Even if my relationship with this person suffers, I will not give in. I cannot compromise on this issue."

Have you ever mourned the loss of a good friend or a job because someone chose to go down a path that was unacceptable to you? Although I have not had to use this style often, I do have areas in my life where I am willing to draw a line in the sand. I was once the CEO of a large graphics company in Florida and stressed for days before firing a key employee who compromised one of our core values.

5. **Partner in the Situation**

The partner is someone who is convinced, until proven otherwise, that problems can and will be solved. She embraces conflict as an opportunity to learn something about herself and the other person. She is a master at what I call the "third idea." When stuck in "my way" or "your way," she sees a new way. She deals with conflict constructively and tries to find a resolution that preserves the dignity of all involved. The partner says, "I care about you and I also care deeply about this issue."

Most Appropriate Style?

Each of these conflict–management styles has positive and negative aspects. Depending on the situation, one may be more appropriate than another. Let's look at some examples.

Pauline Cowan is a friend and advocate for families in her preschool classroom. She deals with conflict using a partner style. Her supervising teacher, Judith Hiscock, says that Pauline speaks out when necessary, but she is so gracious in her approach that conflict rarely escalates.

Nevertheless, Pauline contends that eventually stressful conflicts are bound to happen. In those times, she steps away from the situation and sorts out the facts. "I try to look at the other person's point of view. I like to think before I speak. Sometimes I may not have a chance to sit back and think, so I say a prayer real fast." Pauline's comment reminds me of Abe Lincoln's prayer: "Lord, make my words soft and tender, for tomorrow I may have to eat them."

Although Pauline does not want to offend anyone or make matters worse, she does not shy away from difficult conversations when necessary. "It may hurt to hear it right then, but if I need to speak up, I go ahead. And if it turns out that I did not say the right thing, I can always go back and say, I'm sorry. I made a mistake. Let's start over. Let's discuss this again. If we can talk the situation over, everybody feels better about it. We don't always agree, but we can work together to handle situations positively."

Sometimes it is best to withdraw—at least long enough to think things through. But we shouldn't hesitate to respond in a more controlling manner when the situation demands it.

Vie is one of those people who likes to avoid conflict (withdrawal) if she cannot resolve it through compromise. Leaving the classroom and moving to elementary administration was an exciting time for her—until she discovered it was impossible to please everyone all the time. In her classroom she had an assistant, students, parents, and resource teachers to work with, and conflicts were usually resolved to everyone's satisfaction. When she moved into administration, she had the entire staff, student body, and all the families to work with as well as the central office.

No matter how hard she tried to orchestrate win/win situations, someone grumbled. If she pleased the fifth–grade team with the schedule for music, art, and gym, the third–grade team was not satisfied. If she pleased the third–grade team, first and fifth grades were upset with the schedule. In situations like scheduling, compromises and special classroom needs are considered, but the final decision will not satisfy everyone. Therefore, Vie had to choose a more controlling style.

Probably the greatest lesson Vie learned was that most important decisions do not have to be made on the spot. She found an acceptable comfort level when she could take time to gather information and consider the consequences of different actions before she made a decision. She also learned that it is okay to make a mistake (and to admit it), and that depending on the situation, some decisions needed to be made using a conflict–management style that is outside her preferred style.

Think of a recent conflict in your life. Which conflict–management style did you use? What did you say or do? What was the outcome? Do you think a different style might have worked better in that situation?

Whatever your conflict–management style, there will be situations where a different approach is better. If control is your management style, have you ever wished that you had not spouted off so quickly? When you take time to consider all the aspects before speaking, you may find that your response is more appropriate and better accepted by the listener.

Some conflicts are best smoothed over. Maybe you have heard the saying, "Pick your battles." Be sure the conflict is worthy of addressing before jumping in, but do not smooth over situations that still make you simmer on the inside.

Perhaps you have been in conflict situations where the group is unable to come to a consensus. It is as if the whole team is looking for someone to step up to the plate and assertively make a decision or at least provide direction. In your heart, you know you have the answer or the solution. During times like this, take a deep breath and speak up. Get the team off the fence and moving again. You are not being aggressive, just assertive.

It would be great if every conflict ended in a win/win or partner situation, but that is not going to happen. Even people with the same personality styles will have disagreements among themselves. *Our differences make us both interesting and challenging! How we deal with those differences can destroy our relationships or make them stronger.* Sometimes you can do all the right things and still end up with the wrong results. It does take two to tango (and to tangle), and some people are not just different—they are difficult. I once heard that "It is not the lumps and bumps in life that bother us, it is the jerks." Some people are jerks. You, however, are a professional and will respond rather than react. You will sleep well knowing that you have been a classy communicator.

Don CeSar to the Rescue!

Never cut what you can untie.
—Joseph Joubert

The Don CeSar technique that we learned in chapter five is an excellent way to communicate in a conflict situation, no matter which management style you prefer.
Let's consider this example: A bus driver is confronting a parent who was late meeting the bus. This is the third time the situation has occurred over the past few weeks. The first two times, the driver simply accepted the parent's excuse and apology. In the following confrontation, look for the four parts of the Don CeSar—the event, how it makes the driver feel, why it makes him feel that way, and a follow–up question to find a resolution:

"Oh, sorry I'm late again. I was getting my nails done, and then the traffic was backed up behind a tractor, and—"

"When there is no one here to meet the bus, I feel anxious, because I cannot leave Juan without an adult being home. I am also late delivering the other children when I have to wait. How can we prevent this from happening again?"

People are not upset by what you say, but how you say it. Remember that a key part of the Don CeSar is to use "I–messages" instead of finger pointing with "you–statements." The Don CeSar states the problem in a manner that does not escalate the situation. Some words trigger negative responses, especially in a conflict situation. Try to avoid these escalating words:

- you
- but

- never
- why
- can't
- always
- should

In other words, "You shall not *should* on others." How you deal with conflict will leave everyone involved feeling either bitter or better. By focusing on the problem rather than the person, you do not alienate others. When you describe the behavior rather than attacking the character, you do not escalate the situation. When you state the facts instead of guessing at the motive, your words cannot be challenged.

Look again at the scenario with the bus driver and the late parent. This time the driver is angry and does not communicate in an effective manner:

> *"Oh, sorry I'm late again. I was getting my nails done, and then the traffic was backed up behind a tractor, and–"*

> *"You are always late. What kind of a mother is never here to meet her child? You care more about how you look than you care about your son. You should consider the other children on the route too. You make your child wait, you make me wait, and you make the other children late getting home. If this happens again, I am going to report you to the school."*

Even if the parent is at fault, which conversation is more likely to gain her cooperation in being more responsible in the future?

Engaged Ambassadors Handle Conflict Constructively

Conflict is inevitable. How conflict is handled can destroy or strengthen a team. When we are unable or unwilling to work through conflict, we sacrifice relationships with those around us.

Disengaged Employees	Engaged Ambassadors
☒ Sacrifice relationships in an effort to win the conflict	☑ Seek positive solutions to conflict
☒ Are only concerned with self–satisfaction in conflict resolution	☑ Consider the impact on others
☒ Use one conflict–management style in all situations	☑ Adjust their conflict–management style to the situation

CHAPTER EIGHT

THE DANGER
OF ANGER

*Anger ventilated often hurries toward forgiveness;
and concealed often hardens into revenge.*
—*Edward G. Bulwer–Lytton*

Anger likes to hang around conflict. Where there is conflict, you will probably find anger openly cheering it on, or hiding in the shadows egging it on. Have you noticed that anger is just one letter short of danger? Anger can be a deadly emotion if we do not learn how to handle it. Just as different people have preferred conflict–management styles, they also have anger–management styles.

Ways to Handle Anger

1. **Suppress it**
   Suppression occurs when we stuff anger inside and deny that we are angry.
2. **Express it**
   Expression occurs when we erupt—or just let it all spew out—without thought of how that will affect anyone else.
3. **Confess it**
   Confession occurs when we acknowledge that we are angry, but then find a constructive way to deal with it.

If we pretend that we have no anger and try to bury it, it can bury us (literally) by triggering a heart attack or a stroke. The human body has a physiological response to anger: the pupils dilate; blood sugar rises; blood pressure goes up; muscles tighten and blood clots faster; digestion and elimination slow down; adrenaline flows; respiration speeds up and brings more oxygen to the brain; the heart rate increases; the hypothalamus and pituitary gland become more active.

Letting anger out in the wrong way can ruin our marriage, alienate us from friends, or get us fired. If we turn it around on ourselves, anger can set us up for all kinds of psychological pain. We end up bitter, hostile, and nearly impossible to be around. So what is a person to do? How can you express your anger in a healthy way that does not hurt other people? You can start by asking yourself these questions outlined in William Glasser's book *Reality Therapy.*

1. Why am I angry?
2. What do I want from this conflict?
3. Is what I am doing now helping or hurting my goal?

These are great questions because they get us out of "stewing" and into "doing."

First, why am I angry? In other words, what is the *real* issue here? Many times, we are so angry that we cannot think straight. All the blood rushes from our brains as our bodies prepare for either fight or flight. We cannot answer this first question without putting our brains into gear.

Second, what do I want from this conflict? An apology? A changed behavior? Simply for someone to understand my side of the story? As someone who has done a substantial amount of counseling, I can tell you that many people walk into my office angry, but without a clue as to what they want from this "energy."

Third, is what I am doing *now* helping or hurting? This is the clincher. Whenever I ask myself this question, the answer is normally "hurting." I may be pouting; being passive aggressive, hoping the person I am mad at can get out the crystal ball and know that I am upset and will feel bad about it. There is nothing productive about that behavior!

Why Are You Mad at Me?

He who angers you conquers you.
—Elizabeth Kenny

How do you stay cool, calm, and collected when a coworker, student, or parent is erupting in anger? Maybe you cannot sign them up for a quick course in the Don CeSar method, but you can use your knowledge and skills to respond in a mature and controlled way.

Seventy percent of all anger is displaced anger. Let's look at four common situations that may cause displaced anger.

Causes of Displaced Anger

1. **Fatigue**
    When people are tired, they lose patience easily and may be quick to display anger.
2. **Lack of Control**
    When people lose control of situations, they become frustrated and angry.
3. **Stressful Relationships**
    When relationships are stressful, people often get angry.
4. **Financial Pressure**
    When people feel a threat to their survival or security needs, they are likely to have a short fuse. I like how one teacher put it: "When your outgo exceeds your income, your upkeep becomes your downfall."

When you realize that most anger is displaced, you do not take the attack personally. You can be more empathetic, and you can choose to respond in a mature manner, confronting the problem and not the person. When you do this, you will experience an inner peace and confidence in even the most emotionally charged situations.

What can you do to de–escalate an angry person? Buy some time. Try saying something like this: "I am not sure how to respond to what you have just said. I would like to think about my answer. Are you free to meet this afternoon at two?"

You do not have to attend every fight you are invited to. When ambushed or blind–sided by someone attacking you, you have every right to take a deep breath and allow your brain to kick into gear.

Over the years, I have gathered a list of questions I like to ask myself as a conflict unfolds. These questions will help you as well.

*   Is this person in reasonable shape to discuss the problem? Timing is everything.
*   Can the person or team do anything about the problem? If not, move on.
*   Do we have enough time to work through the situation? If not, schedule time for a crucial conversation.

- Am I in reasonable shape to discuss the problem? If not, ask permission to address it later.
- Can the discussion take place somewhere that will be private and uninterrupted? Typically, the more people dragged into a personal conflict, the messier it becomes.
- What else is happening now? Is the person feeling loss of control, fatigue, or other stresses?

If you feel comfortable dealing with the situation after asking those questions, jump in and be a classy communicator.

Front Line Defense

Am I not destroying my enemies when I make friends of them?
— Abraham Lincoln

School secretaries and receptionists are on the front line when an angry parent phones or storms into the office. Melody Sankey listens, then calmly responds to an irate person in the office. Her principal, Scott Shoop, says, "A couple of years ago we had a new family in the school. They were convinced that I was the enemy, but they saw Melody as an advocate. They have moved from our district, but they still send Melody gifts. She didn't always agree with them, but she always listened to what they had to say."

Melody was an Engaged Ambassador for her school at a time when her principal was unable to make everyone happy with his decisions. Melody did not take sides. She did not make disparaging remarks about anyone or the situation. Melody just listened and showed the family that she cared about them. Melody's principal cared about the family, too, but they were too angry to be able to see his concern. Sometimes a support person will be the only person a family will relate to. That support person just might be *you* — the Engaged Ambassador for your school.

Engaged Ambassadors Deal with Anger Constructively

When you have to deal with others who are angry, remember that most anger is displaced. The way you respond to an angry person will determine if the situation escalates or settles.

Disengaged Employees	Engaged Ambassadors
☒ Fight anger with anger	☑ Admit they are angry
☒ Explode emotionally	☑ Seek the root cause
☒ React without consideration of consequences	☑ Respond rationally and intentionally
☒ Assume malicious intent	☑ Seek to understand the circumstances and intent of others
☒ Do not admit that they have any anger	☑ Find constructive ways to vent
☒ Allow anger over one situation to infect other situations	☑ Use techniques that de–escalate and diffuse

CHAPTER NINE

CHANGE: REACT WITH REASON INSTEAD OF RESISTANCE

> *Change is the law of life and those who look only to the past or present are certain to miss the future.*
> *— John F. Kennedy*

Custodian John Dorman admits that he has a hard time accepting change. John says, "I get set in my ways, but I've learned to deal with change. It's like when the principal transfers or retires, I have to open myself up so I can meet the new principal's needs. You know, not all captains run the ship the same way. People are different in the way they see and do things."

Few people like change. We become comfortable with the familiar and resistant to the unfamiliar. When computers first came into the schools, many staff members were resistant to giving up their electric typewriters. If these employees came to school next Monday and found typewriters instead of computers on their desks, we would have a rebellion!

In the 1970s, only a few people had mobile phones. They were cumbersome contraptions that needed a special antenna attached to the vehicle. Computers filled whole rooms and were not available for personal use. Today cell phones fit in the palm of your hand or nestle in your ear, and they can access the Internet. We have desktop, laptop, notebook, and handheld computers. We have MP3 players, satellite and digital TV, and GPS units. The technology field is changing so rapidly that this list may be obsolete by the time you read this book. Nevertheless, all these tools represent change that many people initially resisted.

Begin at the End

Change is hard because people overestimate the value of what they have—and underestimate the value of what they may gain by giving that up.
—James Belasco and Ralph Stayer,
Flight of the Buffalo

Change occurs when you stop one thing and begin a new one. Ending or letting go of the old is the first step in moving forward.

Leaving the familiar is always difficult. Most people would say that the hardest part of moving to a new town is leaving their old friends behind. When change occurs, you may have something taken away from you. It is a natural thing to feel confused, sad, or even angry. When you initiate change, you probably still feel some of the same emotions, but when you face unwanted change, you may feel like you have little or no control over the situation.

Val Larson, a change–management professional, developed the following model to represent the stages of change.

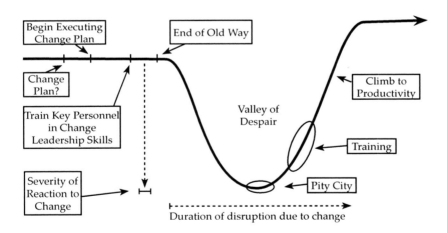

© *Bridges, Enhancements from Val Larson, 2002, © i Six Sigma LLC 2002*

According to Larson's diagram, ending the old way precedes a plunge into the Valley of Despair. In their article, "Developing Black Belt Change Agents," Larson and Mike Carnell say that even if team members accept the change, they will face the Valley of Despair, because "the old way has ended; people are not used to dealing with the ambiguity of the new unknown. They have no recognizable patterns of acting that tell them the 'correct' way to do their job. They need time and help to find their way."

Look at Larson's model again. At the bottom of the valley, you will see Pity City. Have you ever been there? That is the place where people grumble and gripe over the change. Larson and Carnell point out that this is a normal stage and can even be "therapeutic as they swap war stories about the ambiguity and the difficulty they face."

The Valley of Despair is inevitable. Visiting Pity City is normal, maybe even therapeutic. But who wants to stay in such a gloomy place for long? It is time to head up that hill. Use whatever resources you have available to learn about the change. If your change involves new equipment, read the manuals. If you face a new computer program, take the time to work through the tutorials. If your district offers training classes or mentors, take advantage of the opportunity. Knowledge is power, especially during a change situation. The more you understand the change, the less threatening it will seem. Team members can help one another deal with change by sharing information that they have learned.

Rein in Resistance

Nothing is easy to the unwilling.
— *Thomas Fuller*

North Penn High School (Pennsylvania) facilities supervisor Keith Seifert works with twenty–nine custodians in his building. He says that change can range from switching cleaning products to having a new principal on staff. "Accepting change really comes down to respect for the administration," Keith says. "Sometimes they are making a change for a reason I may not be aware of."

Keith makes a great point: lack of knowledge leads to resistance. If you need more information, research the situation or ask your supervisor for clarification. The following questions will help you gather more information for yourself and share that information with your teammates.

- Why is the change needed?
- What is the goal of the change?

- How will this improve the education of the students?
- How will the change affect my team and me?
- What outcomes will this change bring about?
- What support will the school system provide during the transition?

It is important for you to understand the reasons, the anticipated outcomes, and the support you can expect in implementing change. This knowledge will help you and your team members make the climb out of Pity City and on toward embracing the change.

The Revolving Door

The best way out is always through.
—Robert Frost

Secretary Joan Kellner has worked with five principals in her nineteen years at C. G. Stangel Elementary School (Manitowoc Public Schools, Wisconsin). Custodians Barry Crocker and John Dorman have also faced many principal changes in their schools. Secretary Cheryl Jalanivich has worked with three superintendents. Sometimes administrative personnel changes can make a school seem like a revolving door!

It may not be scientific, but in interviewing support staff for this book, it seems that they tend to stay in one location longer than principals and assistant principals. Administrators and teachers frequently move from school to school, and central office staff may change even more. It is no wonder that support personnel do not like change. They have gone through a lot of it! It is easy to understand how a long–time staff member feels when he or she must adjust to principal number five or six. Here comes another new principal who has "great ideas" about new systems and processes. The natural tendency is to say, "I was here before you came, and I'll be here after you leave, thank you." When the support person becomes cynical and calloused, he or she generates negativity, and this affects the entire team. Instead of being the cynical staff member, choose to be the encouraging member, the Engaged Ambassador.

"Cheryl Jalanivich's world was turned upside–down when I showed up," says Superintendent Robert Hirsch. "The previous superintendent was much more elegant, eloquent, and reserved. I am highly excitable and easily stimulated. I wanted my staff to be out in the buildings, on the campuses, and around the kids. I was a high–school principal in the district before becoming superintendent, so I knew Cheryl and I saw her in a professional light as the superintendent's secretary. I was concerned at how she would react to such a change in work climate, but she has done a wonderful job."

Cheryl agrees that the first year working for Mr. Hirsch was a change. "I am flexible and open to new ideas, though. It has been a positive experience, as Mr. Hirsch opened a new area for me — spending time out of the office and in the schools and classrooms. I was hesitant in the beginning, but now I really look forward to it. I might read a story to the children, assist in a classroom, and help in the office. I am getting to know our staff and students face to face. This was a change, but it is very rewarding and something I'm enjoying very much."

Cheryl had also faced change when the previous superintendent came to her district. She says, "He taught me a lot of different things. First, I learned to be flexible. I learned there is more than one way to get the right answer and more than one way to accomplish a task. My job is to support the administrator and other staff members who are overseeing projects that I might assist with. I need to be willing and flexible enough to do it in the manner that they want it done and not be so bullheaded to think that my way is the only way. I am the support person and my job is to support in any way possible."

Secretary Telice Ostrinski says that even a major change can be good, although it might be difficult at first. Telice worked in the Student Assistance Office in San Bernardino, California, for more than nine years and was devoted to her boss, Karen Wilson. When Karen left for a work–from–home position, Telice had the opportunity to take a job with the newly created Family Resource Center. She says, "Making the decision to change was tumultuous. Because I was so close to Karen, I thought I would never have that type of working relationship again. I was very comfortable with her; she treated me like a peer and valued my input. I had my place in that office. I knew exactly what I needed to do."

Karen encouraged Telice and reminded her that the new job would be an opportunity to shine. Telice had mastered skills and procedures in the Student Assistance Office that would be useful in the Family Resource Center. She was a self–starter who always figured out how to do things. Karen knew that Telice was ready for the challenge.

Telice says, "I made the move thinking it would not kill me—and if it was too awful, I could always try something else later." She chuckles as she continues, "It took me about four days to settle into the new job. But I've been able to use my skills and I've learned a lot just being here. Ultimately, change is good, because you learn from change."

Secretary Joan Kellner has been the only constant in the office of Stangel School for the past nineteen years. She shares her secret of working with five principals during that time: "Of course, they all had different personalities and different ways they wanted things done, so I have become quite flexible with change. I have always believed that every single one of us can find new and better ways to do things, and you don't know what works best unless you are willing to try new things. If we try and the old way was better, I would not have a problem suggesting we reconsider the old way—but only after giving the new way a fair chance. I have seen people who get set in their ways and I don't admire that, so I try not to be like that."

Joan's current principal, Debby Shimanek, says that Joan is a reflective person who looks at procedures and analyzes what worked and did not work. For instance, Joan started a list of things that did not go smoothly with the field–trip procedures and made suggestions on ways that might be more efficient next year. Debby says, "I always feel like her goal is to find ways we can get better. Joan embraces change and seeks it out when the old ways do not seem to be the most productive."

Joan's school district transfers employees from one building to another to accommodate enrollment. She understands the pressure and fear that such a move can have on employees, but she says that complaining and threatening to quit are counterproductive—especially when these remarks are made in public. "I believe that employees should not make negative comments in the community. If you enjoy your work, you need to look at the change in a positive way. A transfer to a different location shows that the district values you, and that's better than being laid off." She adds, "You still get to do what you love, just in a different place. And new families will get to enjoy your talents."

When Vie was a teacher, her class relocated from one town in the district to another. Such moves are common in special education, but this time the decision to move the class came four days before school started. The new location was closer to her home, yet her toddler's child–care provider was near the old school. She cried, moaned, and groaned, but only with her trusted team teacher—and only for a few minutes. Yes, she had a private pity party. Remember Larson's Pity City? Then she quickly shifted to a proactive stance. First, calls were made to address her own child–care issues. Then she set to work packing equipment and materials for the move. Was the move hard? You bet. Was it a disaster? Certainly not. Looking back, that move was a positive step in her career and opened up many opportunities she would have missed otherwise.

Changing jobs—even changing jobs within the same district—is stressful. We are not pretending that it is easy. It is normal to grieve leaving old friends and a situation where you are comfortable. A fear of the unknown and the "what ifs" threatened Vie in the building transfer. But by taking a proactive stance and dealing with the details one at a time, the change was manageable.

Who Benefits?

How wonderful it is that nobody need wait a single moment before starting to improve the world.
—Anne Frank

Pauline Cowan says, "No one really likes change unless it benefits them!" Sometimes the benefits are not easy to see at first, so Pauline likes to examine the reason for change and listen to a discussion of pros and cons. "Everything does not always go the way we want it to, but change at school is not about us. We change to benefit our program and our children. That is why I say, if we can sit down and discuss the change, then we can see where it could lead and what it will benefit. We may not always agree with change, but we can work to make it easy on both sides."

Coleen Humberson is the cafeteria manager at Word of God Catholic School (Woodland Hills School District, Pennsylvania). Two weeks before school started in 2006, the venders who created the menus and delivered the food to the school announced that they were no longer able to provide services.

Coleen's principal thought that the students would have to go back to brown–bagging lunches from home. Coleen had other ideas.

"I knew we could do it. I am a risk taker, and it worked out fine. I found a grocery purveyor who was willing to work with me. I found an old set of menus and looked at them. I read all the government information, then started putting menus together."

Coleen's ability to move to a proactive stance resulted in the students having nutritious and delicious hot lunches from the first day of school. Instead of wallowing in Pity City, Coleen learned the basics needed to meet the government requirements for operating a school cafeteria.

She says, "Did you know that there are many types of chicken nuggets? We would start with one brand, and if I did not like the taste of it, we would try another. My feeling was that if my children would not eat it, I was not going to cook it. I even learned that an ice–slush machine—which kids love—could be used with 100 percent fruit." Coleen embraced change positively and proactively in her desire to provide the best benefit for the students.

Nothing Wrong with Being Realistic

If you don't like something, change it.
If you can't change it, change your attitude.
Don't complain.
—*Maya Angelou*

Yes, it is okay to be realistic about the impact that change may have on you. Perhaps it takes more time to work out all the bugs than your supervisor thought it would. Perhaps there will be extra work to get the change implemented. Expect these hurdles as you climb out of the Valley of Despair. Pretending that they are not there is just as unproductive as refusing to overcome them. However, do not become cynical. When you take the smallest step toward understanding and giving change a chance, you will be recognized as an Engaged Ambassador who plans for the pitfalls while moving toward the possibilities.

What should you do if you still feel the change is not working? Talk to your supervisor and explain your reasons for disagreement. Leaders are not always right. Follow the advice of the late John Gardner, a leadership guru and advisor to five former United States presidents, and do not be an unloving critic or an uncritical lover. The main thing is to state your case in a way that does not point fingers.

Maybe your supervisor will reverse the decisions, but if not, move forward making the best of the situation.

How to Invite Change and Have the Boss Eating Out of Your Hand

Everyone thinks of changing the world, but no one thinks of changing himself.
— Tolstoy

You can use change to your own advantage. Most of the time change is thrust upon you, right? Well, what if you invited personal change on the job by asking for honest feedback from your supervisor? Here is how to do it: Schedule a time to sit down and talk with your boss. Ask him or her three questions:

1. What am I doing that you would like me to *stop*?
2. What am I not doing that you would like me to *start*?
3. What am I doing that you would like me to *continue*?

If you approach your boss with this *stop–start–continue* technique, you will have him or her eating out of your hand. It takes courage to invite even constructive criticism, but Engaged Ambassadors are willing to take a risk. When you ask these three questions, you must be ready to receive the responses with open hands. Honestly weigh the information you receive. If it is true, bring it to your heart. If it is not, then let it go. Doing an exercise like this reflects your commitment to being an Engaged Ambassador.

Engaged Ambassadors Embrace Change

Engaged Ambassadors look for the possibilities even when they do not see the positives. They help teammates understand and accept change instead of sabotaging it. They understand that initiating personal change results in growth and gains the respect of supervisors.

How do you respond when faced with change? Can you come up with examples of change that you resisted, but now rely on? When you face change in the workplace, *react with reason instead of resistance.*

Disengaged Employees	Engaged Ambassadors
☒ Resist change	☑ Give change a chance, even if they are unsure about it
☒ Sabotage change efforts	☑ Seek to understand the reason behind the change
☒ Dig their heels in, even when the change is inevitable	☑ Gather and share information about the change
☒ Focus on the reasons that change will not work	☑ Encourage team members during a period of change
☒ Continue to live in the past, long after the train has left the station	☑ Understand that change will have "bumps in the road" during implementation
	☑ See the possibilities instead of the problems

Section 5:

Missions, Goals, and Time Management

CHAPTER TEN

YOUR MISSION...SHOULD YOU AGREE TO ACCEPT IT

My philosophy of life is that if we make up our mind what we are going to make of our lives, then work hard toward that goal, we never lose.
Somehow, we win out.
— Ronald Reagan

A mission statement is a declaration of why an organization or entity exists. I am confident that your district and your school have written missions. Teams and individuals can also have mission statements. All of these must be compatible with one another.

Mission statements within a district are like the front end of a car — poor alignment leads to unacceptable performance. If you are not in agreement with the mission statement of your team or district, then you are in for a bumpy ride.

Alignment in Action

The secret of success is constancy to purpose.
— Benjamin Disraeli

In the next few pages, I will demonstrate the power of purpose by showing how a clear, compelling, and aligned mission motivates. Let's begin by looking at sample mission statements all the way from the district level to the personal level.

District Mission Statement
Adapted from Loudoun County Public Schools, Virginia

- work closely with families and the community
- provide safe schools
- provide a climate in which students can succeed
- provide excellent education that includes academic growth, student responsibility, and respect for others

- promote the moral, ethical, and social development of students.

School Mission Statement
Adapted from Round Hill Elementary School, Nancy McManus, principal

The wording here is different, but the concepts *align* with the district's mission.

To empower students to become responsible and productive citizens of the world, we will:

- provide all students with a positive and challenging learning climate
- partner with families and the community to develop the social, academic, and physical development of the students
- develop critical thinking skills using literacy, the arts, math, science, and technology
- respond to the changes in the family, community, and world.

Individual Teacher's Mission Statement
Adapted from Jennifer Jewell, teacher

My mission is to:

- form a partnership with parents and the community
- prepare my students to become life–long learners
- provide a nurturing, safe environment with high expectations, so students can become responsible, productive citizens in an ever–changing society.

Now if districts, schools, and teachers have mission statements, why not your support team? The same principles apply for everyone—both instructional and non–instructional. Let's look at several examples of how support teams might construct their mission statements.

Transportation Team Mission Statement

Because we believe that safe and timely transportation to and from school is important to ensure that children are in class and ready to learn, our mission is to:

- complete a bus safety check before each run
- complete a bus "sleeping student" check after each run
- request information and follow procedures for health, behavior, and other special needs of the students
- partner with parents to ensure safe bus stop behaviors
- deal with all bus issues (such as complimenting good citizenship or handling discipline) in a positive, respectful, and confidential manner
- partner with school staff to support classroom transportation and safety units by volunteering to speak to the classroom and conducting bus evacuation drills
- encourage student responsibility in following bus safety habits using incentives such as posting student created safety signs.

Clinic Team Mission Statement

Because we believe that students learn best when they are well and in the classroom, our mission is to:

- treat all students in a kind and respectful manner
- handle minor injuries and illnesses in a timely fashion so that students get back to class as soon as possible
- contact parents when students have been treated or need to be sent home
- inform parents of potential health risks and contagious illnesses in the school
- administer medication according to the protocols established by the district
- perform vision and hearing screenings
- review student records for appropriate immunizations and physicals as required by the state
- partner with classroom teachers by providing resources for health and safety units.

Cafeteria Mission Statement

Because we believe that good nutrition contributes to learning, and that the cafeteria provides a natural environment for children to practice skills taught in the classroom, our mission is to:

- provide the students and staff with healthy meals using the county–wide menus
- maintain a clean kitchen and cafeteria area by disinfecting daily and between classes using the same lunch tables
- encourage student independence and responsibility in lunch procedures, but being available to assist when needed
- foster good relationships with students and parents by dealing with any issues (allergies, lost lunch money, and overdue lunch payments) in a positive, respectful, and confidential manner
- develop good parent and community relationships by welcoming visitors to join students for lunch
- partner with teachers and other staff to help students develop healthy habits and choices relative to food and nutrition.

A problem with alignment can occur if an individual does not buy into the mission statement of the team. Perhaps the cafeteria cashier is not positive with the children and is impatient if they do not have their lunch money or prepaid ticket ready when they get to the register. Even worse, if a child owes charges, this cashier embarrasses the child over the issue and makes comments loud enough for other students to hear. This cashier is not treating the students in a respectful and confidential manner. When an employee fails to align with the team's mission, sometimes it is because he or she is only working for a paycheck and has no passion for the job.

Spending Some Time at MGM

The tragedy of life doesn't lie in not reaching your goal.
The tragedy lies in having no goals to reach.
—Benjamin Mays

When I lived in Florida, I frequently took out–of–town visitors to Metro–Goldwyn–Mayer studios. The acronym MGM reminds me that a mission statement generates goals, and these need to be measurable. So I use MGM to represent *Mission/Goals/Measurable*.

If the custodial mission statement included "Create community pride in the school by improving the curb appeal of the building," the goals might include:

- Mow the lawn weekly.
- Walk the grounds each morning to check for litter.
- Remove weeds from the mulched areas weekly.
- Clean the glass in the doors daily.
- Collaborate with the Life Science teacher to include students in planting and caring for annuals each spring.

The cafeteria mission statement referenced earlier might include these goals:

- Wash the lunch tables with a bleach solution between classes.
- Clean all spills immediately.
- Provide table awards for good cafeteria manners each week.
- Assist third–grade grade teachers with their classroom vegetable garden by planning and supervising students in maintaining a compost pile with cafeteria scraps.

These goals are focused and measurable. Measurement can be as simple as using a checklist. The thesaurus gives these other words for measurable: *quantifiable, assessable, able to be gauged, computable, calculable*, and *reckonable*. Ask yourself, "Am I able to determine whether I've completed the goal?" If you can answer yes, your goal is measurable.

Engaged Ambassadors are Mission Minded

Does your team have a written mission? If not, lead the way by facilitating its creation. Remind them that putting beliefs, values, and purposes in writing is a powerful tool for building internal team focus and for communicating to external customers. Someone once asked Helen Keller what was worse than being blind. Her response was "having sight, but no vision."

Your team mission needs to be supported with measurable

goals. In his teleseminar, Brian Tracy says that successful people spend 80 percent of their time focusing on plans, goals, and passions; those in the other camp spend 80 percent of their time focusing on the problems, challenges, and setbacks. Which camp do you choose to join?

Disengaged Employees	Engaged Ambassadors
☒ Are not aware of, or interested in, the district or school's mission and goals	☑ Believe in and help shape the mission of the team
☒ Work day to day, without a plan for the future	☑ Understand how to support the team mission
☒ Believe that goal setting wastes time instead of saves time	☑ Have personal mission statements
	☑ Support their mission statements with measurable goals
	☑ Set personal goals and plan steps to attain them

CHAPTER ELEVEN

NOW?
OR LATER?

> Time is the stuff which life is made of.
> To waste your time is to waste your life.
> To master your time is to control your life.
> —Benjamin Franklin

As I travel across the country speaking at schools, the number–one complaint I hear from support staff is lack of time. Your plate is full. You feel overwhelmed before you even start the day, and sometimes defeated at the end of the day because you have not made a dent in your list of things to do. Often the question is not whether your calendar will be full, but who will fill your calendar.

You now understand the importance of your mission and setting goals. The next challenge is having the time–management tools necessary to accomplish them. Dealing with interruptions, focusing on the important tasks, and overcoming procrastination are a few of the battles all professionals must fight.

Taming the Tiger

> The weakest creature, by concentrating his powers on a single object, can accomplish something; whereas the strongest, by dispersing his over many, may fail to accomplish anything.
> —Thomas Carlyle

Do you know why animal trainers carry a stool when they go into a cage of tigers? The trainer holds the stool by the back and thrusts the legs toward the face of the wild animal. Trainers maintain that the tiger tries to focus on all four legs at once. In the attempt to focus on all four, a kind of paralysis overwhelms the animal. It becomes tame, weak, and disabled because its attention is fragmented.

Have you ever had so much coming at you during the day that you did not know where to start? Like the tiger and the stool legs, you may be overwhelmed with many trivial tasks rather than a few important ones. By focusing on what is important and prioritizing your tasks, you will move to the head of the pack and complete your goals.

Delight Creech, Communities in Schools director for Hudson Area Schools (Michigan), knows how to focus on what is important. She is responsible for working with schools, families, and the community. She describes her job as finding what the needs of the school district are and then matching resources in the community to those needs. Her responsibility ranges from assisting a family with food and clothing to setting up school and business partnerships. Delight also heads up the crisis–intervention team for the school district. It would be easy to forget something while juggling several projects at once, so Delight uses her Palm Pilot® and a planner. She chuckles as she says, "When you get older, your memory starts to fade, so I have to have things written down." Delight prioritizes the projects. She then breaks each one down into manageable goals and tackles them one step at a time.

Lions on the Loose

Keep focused on substantive issues. To make a decision means having to go through one door and closing all others.

— Abraham Zaleznik

In *First Things First* (Covey, Merrill, and Merrill, 1994), the authors provide a method to help you prioritize your responsibilities. They categorize tasks into four quadrants based on whether they are important or urgent.

	Urgent	Not Urgent
Important	**I** • Crises • Pressing problems • Deadline–driven projects, meetings, preparations	**II** • Preparation • Prevention • Values Clarification • Planning • Relationship Building • True Re–Creation • Empowerment
Not Important	**III** • Interruptions, Some Phone Calls • Some Mail, Some Reports • Some Meetings • Many Proximate, Pressing Matters • Many Popular Activities	**IV** • Trivia, Busywork • Junk Mail • Some Phone Calls • Time Wasters • "Escape" Activities

©1994 *Covey Leadership Center, Inc. (used by permission)*

1. **Important and Urgent**

    These tasks demand immediate attention. They are both important and urgent. If a lion walked into the school, you would have to drop whatever you were doing to help deal with the situation. Okay, that is not likely to happen, but the letters l–i–o–n can stand for "Like It Or Not!" When those important and urgent tasks interrupt your schedule, you have to deal with them immediately, whether you like it or not.

2. **Important and Not Urgent**

    You have control over these tasks. Instead of the task acting upon you (like the l–i–o–n), you take action on the task. You must be proactive with these important but not urgent tasks. These tasks should be taking up most of your workday and will move you toward completion of your goals.

3. **Urgent and Not Important**

    Do you sometimes feel that bothersome little tasks need immediate attention? The key word here is *feel*. You have to determine if the task is one of the trivial many, or one of the critical few that must be addressed right away. These tasks are easy to take care of but do not really move you forward with your goals.

4. **Not Urgent and Not Important**

   Some workers spend their time stewing over things they cannot control or things that are time wasters. Let those things go. Spend your time on tasks that move you toward your goal.

Handling Interruptions with M&Ms

If you chase two rabbits, both will escape.
— Unknown

Interruptions often start with the question "Do you have a minute?" Well, nothing works better with interruptions than plain old M&Ms. No, I am not talking about the Mars brand candy, although that might not be such a bad idea. Hmm. "Take two of these and see me about that later."

M&M stands for Minimize and Manage. We average fifty interruptions per day. If you can eliminate just one minute from the time you give each one, you will gain almost an hour.

You have the best of intentions to complete your important tasks, but interruptions pop up like wildfires, and you are off to the rescue. Whew! You saved the day, but your reports are still not done. Real fires need attention (remember the l–i–o–n), but the "fires" are often false alarms.

Here are some pointers to help you Minimize and Manage interruptions:

1. **Determine the type of interruption.**
   - Unnecessary—The interrupter mistakenly assumes you have the required information to address a matter or that you are responsible for the situation.
   - Necessary—You do have the required information and are responsible for dealing with the situation. This is a l–i–o–n and must be dealt with as soon as possible.
   - Necessary, but Untimely—You do need to take care of the interruption, but not at this time. This is where you learn to prioritize and not assume that every fire is burning out of control. Some fires can burn awhile

and present no danger unless they get you sidetracked off a critical task.

2. **Use questions to help your coworker get to the point.**
   Let's say, someone interrupts your work and begins to engage in unrelated conversation. You want to be friendly, so you listen, but then you might ask, "Is there something I can do for you?" This allows you to be courteous—which is good customer service—but also allows you to determine if this person has a job–related reason for the interruption.

3. **Interrupt yourself.**
   "I'm sorry, Susan. I just noticed the time. Are there other items we need to discuss?"

4. **Set time limits.**
   "Frank, I have five minutes now or thirty minutes later today. Which do you prefer?"

5. **Phone interruptions:**
   "I'd better let you go," or,"Why don't I get started on this now?"

Preventative Maintenance

One thing you can't recycle is wasted time.
—Unknown

Scheduling regular meetings with your teammates will eliminate many interruptions and take care of potential problems before they become time–consuming major issues.

Custodian Barry Crocker meets with his staff right after the student breakfast duties are completed. He says, "I tell them what's going on with the night shift—if there is a meeting happening that night and other things on the schedule. I ask if they have any problems that I can help with. One custodian might tell me a teacher's class is always messy. It takes me just a few minutes to go down and talk to the teacher, or I can stop by at bell time and ask the students to pick up a little more."

Carmen Duran, building supervisor for Northside Elementary (Elko County School District, Nevada) often teams with the school secretary, Linda West, in determining what tasks are most important for the day. Carmen says, "Linda and I both get here about six in the morning, and we'll work out a list of the things that need to be done first that day."

Secretary Joan Kellner and her principal, Debby Shimanek, sit down together and figure out the priorities for the day. Debby says, "If Joan has a report due, I'll give her time to do it. She also reminds me of things I need to do that day. Joan is learning to delegate some of the jobs to the new office assistant/health aide. We talk about what jobs she could give up or share with this person. Sharing responsibilities strengthens the sense of team and trust for the new employee. It is like saying, 'I know you will get this done, I trust you to take care of it.'"

Sometimes You Just Have to Deal with It

I learned that we can do anything, but we can't do everything...at least not at the same time. So think of your priorities not in terms of what activities you do, but when you do them. Timing is everything.
— Dan Millman

Custodian John Dorman says that interruptions are going to happen and you just have to deal with them. He carries a small notepad and a pen in his pocket and tries to write down requests throughout the day. He says, "I prioritize. If there is something I can put off because other jobs need to be taken care of first, I do that. I mark my list 1–2–3–4 by priority, and I mark items off as I complete them." He chuckles and adds, "There are days that are so busy that requests can totally leave my mind. So I always tell people, if they don't hear back from me by the end of the day don't hesitate to whistle, tap me on the shoulder, or leave me a note to remind me."

Secretary Melody Sankey single–handedly runs the busy Newcastle Middle School office. She alerts visitors that she may need to answer the phone while helping them, and apologizes in advance. She says, "Most people are very patient while waiting to be helped. My goal is that no one feels I do not have time to help him or her. If the phone does interrupt us, I ask if they will excuse me for a moment."

If you also deal with the one–person office, it may be helpful to prepare a special phone message that lets the caller know that you are assisting someone else and will return his or her call within a few minutes. If that is not possible, be sure to explain to visitors and get their permission to answer the phone, as Melody does.

How does Melody handle necessary but untimely

interruptions? Every school secretary deals with this particular example, but Melody was brave enough to voice it for all the others. Sometimes teachers do not make enough copies of worksheets and do not realize this until they are ready to use the material. They send a child to the office with the urgent request. (Usually they send the melt–your–heart kid with the big smile and twinkling eyes.) In these cases, Melody will put her work aside and make the copies as quickly as possible so instruction is not delayed.

For interruptions that do not directly affect instruction in the classroom, Melody will ask if the person could come back at a certain time. She makes sure they know she cares and wants to help them, and she gets back to them as soon as possible.

I Have Not Yet Begun to Procrastinate

Procrastination means making an appointment with opportunity and then asking her to come around some future time.
                                        — *Reed Smoot*

It is easy to say, "Just do it," but many of us struggle with avoiding certain jobs. Let's look at some of the reasons we put tasks off, and suggestions for getting out of the procrastination trap.

Fear or lack of confidence in your ability to complete a task may be one cause. If you do not have the skill needed, ask for assistance or find out about special training. "How–to" information is readily available on the Internet, and many school systems are providing training for support staff. Some systems will provide tuition help for private coursework. Ask your teammates for help and be willing to help them master a task that you are confident in doing. Often lack of confidence is a perception rather than a reality, and once you get started on a job you will discover that you can do it after all. Hands–on experience is usually the greatest teacher!

Seeking perfection can also cause procrastination. If you do not think you can do the task perfectly, you may avoid doing it at all. If you do start on it, you never finish because it is just not perfect. Schools would come to a complete stop if every task were done perfectly or not at all. Strive for *excellence* instead of *perfection*.

Breaking a task down into small steps is a sound strategy for overcoming procrastination. The task may appear overwhelming, but becomes manageable when it is tackled one step at a time. For example, the clinic assistant or nurse might be required to screen vision and hearing for all the third graders before the end of the first grading quarter. This task might be broken down like this:

- Check with principal and get dates for screening placed on staff calendar.
- Send note to teachers with the dates and specific times for the classes.
- Call the volunteer coordinator to get a parent to assist in shuttling students between classroom and clinic for screening, and one to assist with the testing.
- Order additional screening forms from the central office if needed.
- On the afternoon before screening day, set up the audiometer and the eye charts in the clinic.

Manufacturing a sense of urgency is another effective procrastination buster. Have you noticed that you are most productive the last day of work before your vacation? You want to catch up on your responsibilities before you leave. The urgency of finishing before you leave helps you meet goals quickly. You can create urgency with deadlines by pretending you have a plane to catch. Share your deadline with a teammate. Ask her to hold you accountable for meeting the deadline. You can also put off more pleasant tasks until you have finished a less enjoyable one.

I love to ride horses. When I find myself staring out the window rather than doing my work (like writing this book), I say to myself, *Write fifteen more pages and then you can go to the farm.* I am instantly motivated!

Engaged Ambassadors Manage Time Efficiently

When everything is coming at you at once, focus on what is most important. Refer to the Covey quadrants to help you order your tasks by importance and urgency. When interruptions come (and they will), use your skills to minimize and manage them.

The best time to start using the techniques you have learned in this chapter is now. Tackle procrastination as if it were your greatest enemy. Lee Iacocca said, "If you want to make good use of your time, you've got to know what is most important and then give it all you've got."

Disengaged Employees	Engaged Ambassadors
☒ Work without a plan for the day	☑ Prioritize tasks
☒ Let interruptions guide their activities	☑ Focus on the important and urgent
☒ See all responsibilities and tasks as being equally important	☑ Have a schedule, but are flexible
☒ Put tasks off instead of getting started on them	☑ Anticipate and address situations that may cause interruptions
☒ Grease the squeaky wheel	☑ Minimize and manage interruptions
	☑ Tackle less pleasant tasks without procrastinating

Section 6:

Building Bridges, and a Little Bit More

CHAPTER TWELVE

TOUCHING LIVES, MAKING A DIFFERENCE

A hundred years from now it will not matter what my bank account was, the sort of house I lived in, or the kind of car I drove...but the world may be different because I was important in the life of a child.
— *Forest E. Witcraft*

The above quote is among my favorites. There is no greater legacy than being important in the life of a young person. A smile, an encouraging word, a listening ear—these things show the students in your school that you care about them and believe in them. Who can make a difference in the life of a child? It might just be you.

It Might Just Be Me

Here he comes again, bounding through the door,
Proclaiming his innocence today, once more.
Each day he arrives and takes the same chair,
Facing trouble with a look of "I don't care."

...

I learned with great sadness, when Dad came that day,
That his wife, the boy's mother, had just passed away.
His dad thanked me for all I had done.
His hand on the boy's shoulder, he said, "Let's go home Son."

With no mom by his side to show him the way,
A fractured family would struggle to get through each day.
Who would guide that boy where he needed to be?
I suddenly realized, ***it might just be me.***

—Steve Constantino, 2002

Just Being There

The best and most beautiful things in the world cannot be
seen or even touched. They must be felt with the heart.
                                   —*Helen Keller*

Secretary Joan Kellner was there for a second grader. She says, "This past school year has probably been my hardest because of a little boy who passed away in June, after an eighteen–month battle with cancer. I had become very close to this sweet person because he spent many lunch hours in my office when it was too cold for him to go outside. In his last few weeks, I often went to visit him and his parents after school and on the weekends. My desire now is to remember the parents, although they no longer have a child in our school. They need support and I will continue to help them in any way I can."

Joan was there for this child. She was a bridge of goodwill for the school, and bridges connect in two directions. Joan's life was also touched by the interactions that she shared with this child.

Another student, a little boy with autism, visits Joan in the office twice each morning. First he brings down the lunch slip, and later he brings the milk count. When his aide started bringing him to the office to learn these simple errands, he would not speak. Joan says, "By the end of the school year, he would respond when I said good morning. If I thanked him for bringing me his paperwork, he would respond with 'Thank you, Mrs. Kellber.' I was thrilled to hear him say my name his way, instead of Kellner. When I learned that he liked dinosaurs, I bought a dinosaur book for him at a rummage sale and had it on my desk for him one morning. The look on his face when I gave it to him was priceless."

Joan knows that the small kindness she shows may have a ripple effect, and she wants to make a difference in the lives of the children around her.

A Four–Dollar Legacy

There are two lasting bequests we can give our children:
One is roots. The other is wings.
                                   —*Hodding Carter Jr.*

"Bus 54, where are you?" Jim Murley is the driver of Bus 54 in Waxahachie, Texas. He has good–naturedly suffered through the "bus 54" jokes, and he chuckles as he describes himself as Santa–like, with the belly but not the beard. A few summers ago, Jim wanted to do something for his students. He says, "I wanted to encourage my kids. I wanted them to know they were smart and could achieve great things."

Jim came up with the idea of starting a "Reading Riders" program on his bus. A four–dollar purchase at the dollar store got him forty shiny pencils as prizes. "I told the kids if they read a book on the bus every day for a week, they would get a pencil on Friday. I could not believe how excited they were over those pencils. The first week maybe twelve or fourteen started reading books. The others were asked to talk quietly so they would not disturb the readers. No one had to participate."

The response was overwhelming. Within a couple of weeks, nearly the whole bus was reading. Jim then approached the manager at the local Wal–Mart and explained his program. The store donated a twenty–dollar gift certificate. Jim says, "I went right to the book department and picked out six books. I told the kids that the six who read the most books between then and Thanksgiving would get a brand–new book of their own. When I gave the books to the winners, I wrote a personal note inside each cover, congratulating them and saying I was proud of them."

Jim continued working with local merchants to help supply prizes for the Reading Riders, and the grand finale of the year was a donation of all–day tickets to Six Flags amusement park. Students receive small prizes for each book read, and major prizes are earned for the most books read. The real prize, however, is not a pencil, a book, or even a ticket to Six Flags. The real prize is the lasting relationship that Mr. Jim is developing with the students. As they get on the bus in the mornings, they eagerly show him the books they are reading. When the bus has to wait ten minutes at one of the schools, the students take turns telling Mr. Jim about their books.

Jim constantly reminds his kids that he believes in them. He says, "You guys are so smart. You can read many different things — books, magazines, the newspaper. I know you are going to succeed." He even has a bus cheer that encourages the students: "What bus do the smartest kids ride? Bus 54!"

One of Jim's routes is bilingual, with Spanish being the predominant language. Jim took Spanish classes so he could encourage the children in their primary language. This built relationships with the parents as well, since Mr. Jim could communicate with them. He says, "I'll probably never be fluent, but it gives the parents a warm feeling when I can talk to them and they can understand me."

Jim's greatest joy came when some of the students told him that they had done well on their reading tests in the classroom. Then the teachers started commenting on reading scores going up for several of the Bus 54 Reading Riders. Jim beams and says, "It makes it worthwhile to see the glow in their eyes when they realize they are good readers. I tell them that reading gives them knowledge, and knowledge will give them power to open doors of opportunity."

Jim rarely has discipline issues, but he did have to write up a student for a bus infraction. The young man and his parents ran into Jim in a local store a few days later. Jim took the opportunity to express his feelings about the incident to the parents in front of the boy. "Everyone makes a mistake once in a while. Your son is a very respectful and polite boy. He is also very smart. He made a mistake, but that's over and everything is going to be good."

Jim Murley is making a difference. He is touching lives in a manner that will long outlast the trinkets and amusement–park tickets he gives out for reading. Jim is building strong self–esteem in his students, and even if no one else encourages them, they will never forget the legacy that Mr. Jim provided. They will always know that he believes in them. My guess is that they will live up to his expectations.

A Full Stomach

One word or a pleasing smile is often enough to raise up a saddened and wounded soul.
— St. Theresa of Lisieux

Remember walking into a school and smelling rolls baking? Few school cafeterias still make homemade bread, but cafeteria manager Shirley Anthony continues to practice the art of creating yeast rolls from scratch.

Mrs. Shirley, as the students and staff fondly call her, has a secret ingredient for her melt–in–your–mouth rolls, and she uses it to season all the food cooked at Franklinton Elementary School (Washington Parish, Louisiana). That ingredient is love for the children. She says, "The main thing is to love these children and keep a positive attitude.

You don't know what is going on in their lives, and some of them may not have eaten a meal since you fed them on Friday. When I serve my family, I want to give them a good meal. I tell the people who work with me that we need to cook like we were going to serve it to our families. You have to put love in it. You have to treat these children as though they were your children. We put love in, not just because we work here, but because we care about the children."

Many cafeteria workers look forward to summer vacation, but not Shirley. She worried about the children being hungry when they were not in school. Her district's new nutrition program now allows her to cook for students in a summer reading program, as well as any children in the community who come into the school for meals. Shirley and her team provide breakfast and lunch for the forty summer students plus an additional 140 children from the community. "I'm happy about that because I know these children are eating. A full stomach means a whole lot. You can't learn if you are hungry."

Sometimes Shirley has a child approach her who is still hungry after finishing the meal. Perhaps the child gets free or reduced lunch, or perhaps he or she pays full price. It doesn't matter. Shirley says, "If they don't have any money to buy extra, what are you going to do? I'm not going to say, 'Well baby, you don't have any money. I'm sorry, you can't get anything else.' Of course not. I'm going to go into my purse, or if there is lots of extra food, I give it to him. You have to love these children, because sometimes a lot of things are lacking at home."

Everybody's Mama

I've learned that people will forget what you said, people will forget what you did, but people will never forget how you made them feel.

—Maya Angelou

Sharlene Barrois lost all of her material possessions in Hurricane Katrina. Her parish of Buras was the place where the killer storm made landfall in Louisiana. Sharlene had been the attendance secretary at Buras High School for twenty years when Katrina destroyed the school.

Sharlene relocated to Belle Chasse High School, forty–five miles north of her old school, as did many of the families from Buras.

At first, she was assigned to the district office. She says, "I was happy to know I had a job, but my heart was with the children. I kept telling my boss that I had to get back to my kids. I am sixty–one, but the kids keep me young. Finally I was granted my wish and sent to Belle Chasse High School."

Jemi Carlone is Sharlene's assistant principal. She says, "Many of the children who lost everything in the storm moved up here to Belle Chasse, even now, about 20 percent of our students came from Buras High. Ms. Sharlene is their connection to the school they lost. They will come in the office and say, 'My mom said to tell you hello,' or, 'My uncle is not feeling well.' Sharlene keeps Buras alive for the kids. It is still hard on everybody. That school meant so much to them, and Sharlene keeps those memories and relationships alive. Most of the students whose families relocated are still living in FEMA trailers. These camping–size units may have a family of four or five living in them. In the midst of continuing hardship, Sharlene is a point of hope for the students.

Even before Katrina, Sharlene touched lives. In 2000, the senior class of Buras High School dedicated the yearbook to her. "My biggest surprise ever was when they dedicated the yearbook to me. They called me their mom away from home. They said I was there for all their problems throughout the years. That is why I wanted to be back in the schools. These kids have made my life worth living."

Yes, bridges of goodwill go both ways.

Engaged Ambassadors Make a Difference

You are in a position to make a difference in this world. It only takes a smile, a kind word, and a sincere spirit of caring to make a difference in students' lives and in the future of the world.

Disengaged Employees	Engaged Ambassadors
☒ Do not invest in the success of others	☑ Know that they touch lives
☒ Fail to consider the impact of their actions on those around them	☑ See the best in students and want the students to believe in themselves
☒ Focus on tasks rather than relationships	☑ Encourage students
	☑ Care about others

CHAPTER THIRTEEN

CONFIDENTIALLY:
RESPECT IT AND PROTECT IT

Great people talk about ideas. Small people talk about others.
—unknown

Secretary Debbie Malsack says that good judgment is the key to confidentiality. In her job at Durkee Elementary School (Kenosha Unified School District, Wisconsin), she knows that good judgment includes respect for the feelings, the safety, and the right to privacy for everyone connected to the school.

Imagine how you would feel if the receptionist at your doctor's office chatted to friends about your diagnosis, then told about your child being uncooperative when she had to have blood drawn. Or what if a perspective employer phoned your health–care provider to check up on how often you were sick? We all value our privacy and expect those who work in our health–care facility to treat our information with respect. This is a legal and ethical responsibility of those in the medical profession. The Health Insurance Portability and Accountability Act (HIPAA) of 1996 protects your personally identifiable health information. Medical professionals may not release your past, present, or future health and treatment records or your records of payment for services without your permission. This protection includes informal discussion of your information as well as the sharing of written records.

Legal Protections

Talk is cheap until you hire a lawyer.
—unknown

Schools have similar privacy protections under FERPA, the Family Educational Rights and Privacy Act, also referred to as the

Buckley Amendment of 1974. This federal law protects the privacy of students' educational records and gives parents and eligible students the rights of access to and procedures for amending records. FERPA specifies what student information can be shared and with whom. Only those persons in the school who have a legitimate educational reason to access student records can do so. Teachers have access to their students' records only for the year that they work with those students. A freshman English teacher cannot pull a senior's file just because she taught him in ninth grade. Student records also include classroom information such grades, class work, and disciplinary issues.

Ethical Considerations

> *In our appetite for gossip, we tend to gobble down everything before us, only to find, too late, that it is our ideals we have consumed, and we have not been enlarged by the feasts but only diminished.*
>
> — *Pico Iyer, journalist*

We need to be aware of student legal protections, but let's not stop there. As Engaged Ambassadors, we have a moral and ethical responsibility not to gossip about students, families, teammates, or our supervisors.

Many state boards of education have a code of ethics for their employees. These codes almost universally include a statement that employees shall not disclose information that they have learned about students in the course of their work, unless law requires it. Some support staff members work directly with students; others have opportunities to observe students in places like the hallway, office, or cafeteria. Sharing information in the community about a student's behavior, grades, appearance, or family is inappropriate.

Vie worked with special–needs students in two states and five school systems. Many years ago, she was at a community event and was shocked to hear a woman in the group talking about an unruly student. This woman was an instructional aide in a learning disabilities classroom. She made comments about the child's home life and complained about her supervising teacher. Of course, the listeners were riveted to the stories and contributed their own negative comments about "that student, those awful parents, and the terrible teacher." Then they heaped sympathies on "the poor aide who had to deal with this situation." The woman who was breaking confidentiality did not know that Vie worked for the schools. Well, Vie was less assertive back then, but she did squeak out, "I'm sorry, but I work in the school system, too, and I don't think we should be talking about students in our care."

Several years after that, Vie attended a holiday party and met a friend of the host. This party guest patted Vie on the shoulder and said she had heard about a particular child in Vie's classroom. I am not sure if this woman did not understand body language, but disregarding the look of horror on Vie's face and her stiff posture, the woman continued to describe behaviors that only an insider could have known.

Vie's beloved and trusted classroom assistant turned out to be best friends with the party guest. The assistant was not a bad person; in fact, she was one of the best assistants Vie ever had. She loved the children. She treated them with respect and always saw their abilities rather than their disabilities. However, some of the students had behavioral concerns, and that was the reason they were in the special–needs room. The assistant had not talked maliciously about this child, yet her descriptive comments, shared in confidence with her best friend, were inappropriate. If her friend felt it was okay to discuss the student and classroom with Vie at a party, she would not hesitate to share the information with other people.

Psst! Did You Hear About…

There is so much good in the worst of us, and so much bad in the best of us, that it hardly behooves any of us, to talk about the rest of us.
    —Edward Wallace Hoch (1870–1904)

Support employees are charged with the same standards as certified employees where confidentiality is concerned. We have all been cornered at the gas station or the high–school football game by a curious parent who wants to get the inside information about what is going on "down there at the school." Of course, parents have a right to information concerning their own children and about the school. We encourage parents to be proactive with their children's education, but there are proper channels for them to seek this information. When you find yourself in a situation like this, it is best to refer the parent to the principal or assistant principal. If he or she persists in asking questions, you can politely respond, "I'm not in a position to answer that, but I'll be happy to pass your concerns on to the principal. Let me get your name and phone number."

Let's see how some of our Engaged Ambassadors handle tricky situations involving confidential information.

Pauline Cowan treats confidential information in the same manner that she would want such information handled if it were about her own family. As a pre–kindergarten classroom assistant, Pauline has daily contact with most of the parents, and they often share family information with her.

Pauline's supervising teacher, Judith Hiscock, says, "Pauline does not discuss our students or any other students in the school. When confidential information is shared with her, she never passes it on except when appropriate to the classroom teacher. Pauline does not judge anyone; instead, she tries to help whenever possible. However, if there is a danger to a student or family member, Pauline contacts the appropriate school administrators or officials. She is always trustworthy and dependable."

Opportunities for breaching confidentiality can occur within the schools just as easily as in the community. Pauline is discouraged if she hears gossip going on in the teacher's lounge. She says, "I don't need to be drawn into gossip. If you join in, you will get as deep into it as the others. It's best to keep your mind on what you are supposed to be doing, and that is to be here for the kids." An effective strategy for minimizing gossip is to respond to loose lips by asking, "What is your reason for sharing this with me?" You will be amazed at how this stops gossip in its tracks. Most people will say, "Never mind," then engage in appropriate conversation.

Classroom and cafeteria assistant Marcia Forsythe takes confidential information to the proper channels and nowhere else. She urges caution when engaging in conversations even within the school building since visitors are in and out and may overhear a discussion between professional staff.

Secretary Telice Ostrinsky previously worked in a student assistance office with psychologists, counselors, and a social worker. Many of the parents who called the office were distraught and blurted out details of their situation to anyone who answered the phone. Telice would direct their calls to the person who needed to assist them. She says, "We never discussed issues in the office, and I always maintained the student's private information."

Sometimes Telice's manager, Karen Wilson, needed Telice to help with reports. Karen says, "I knew that all the information I shared with her for the reports would be kept confidential. She knew how to handle the confidentiality involved with phone calls, faxes, and information from Child Protective Services."

Telice also maintained confidentiality outside of the office. On one occasion, a friend phoned to ask a question about an incident in the district's middle school.

"My friend knew I worked with the crisis team in my office. She had heard rumors and called to ask me about an incident. I politely told her that her kids were safe, but other than that, I could not talk about the incident. It might come out in the media later, but no one was going to hear the information from me. My staff knew that if I heard something in the office, it was going to stay in the room."

Secretary Melody Sankey refers inappropriate inquiries from the parents or community to her principal. She says, "I tell them that I can't talk about that, but that they can speak to Mr. Shoop if they have questions or concerns."

Nurse Joanne Jones maintains medical information in a confidential manner. Health records and protocols for students with medical conditions are only shared with those teachers and staff members who work directly with the students. Joanne reminds these staff members that the information is confidential.

Joanne works in a small community and knows most of the parents. Sometimes they ask her questions about other students in the school, but she simply says that she cannot discuss other children with them.

Belva Sarten, health aide in Oroville City Elementary School District (California), spends twenty hours a week working with families in their homes. Her job includes educating families about controlling head lice. We may not like to talk about it, but head lice have been a problem in schools for many years and contribute to high absentee rates. They can strike anyone—they do not respect social class or cleanliness. Yet, there continues to be a stigma associated with lice, and families are embarrassed when these pests infest their homes and children.

Belva approaches her job with compassion and deep concern for helping the families eradicate the lice and for getting the children back in school as soon as possible. She says, "I got lice myself once. It was embarrassing to me, so I know how the kids feel. I love the families and I treat them like I want to be treated. I never look down on anyone because of their circumstances."

Belva sometimes has to deal with situations of abuse and neglect within families. School employees, by law, must report suspected abuse or neglect. "I have to make reports to the authorities, but I do not share this information with anyone except my supervisor. I keep family information confidential. I have gained the trust of the families and I honor that."

Bus driver and classroom aide Sherry Cunningham works with special–needs students. She understands that these students have a legal right to privacy, and she keeps all information from the classroom and the bus confidential.

Since Sherry drives for the students in her classroom, parents ask her questions when she brings their children home. "You really have to be careful what you say, even positive comments may be misinterpreted. Often the parents ask me if their child had a good day. Once I answered this question by saying the child had a great day." When Sherry responded "great day," the parent assumed that none of the other days had been positive. This may sound ridiculous, but Sherry learned that sometimes parents turn words around to support their own ideas. Now Sherry reminds the parents that they are welcome to come by the school and talk to the teacher if they have a concern.

Sherry cautions all staff members about discussing students in the school lounge. "You go in and there is chatter going on, but you need to be careful not to talk about students and confidential issues. Substitute teachers also use the lounge, and they hear what is said and may even repeat it in the community."

Bus driver Stephanie Townsend says, "I send a letter out to my bus parents at the beginning of the school year and include my phone number. They know they can call me anytime with concerns." Sometimes, though, parents call and want details about bus situations that may involve students other than their own. When that happens, Stephanie requests that the parent call the principal.

Secretary Joan Kellner says that staff and students often confide in her. She says, "I am a good listener and give each person the respect of my confidentiality. The first job I had was in an office of a large company where I worked in a steno pool. My supervisor told us to type it and forget it. That was over thirty years ago, but I still abide by that rule, although in the school it's not always things I type, but oftentimes things that I am told."

Cheryl Jalanivich is the secretary for the district's superintendent. Working in the central office, she deals with sensitive information about personnel and students. She says, "It is very important that what happens within the walls of this office remain within the walls of this office. I will not divulge anything that could create problems. I will not share information or even allude to anything that transpires here."

Cheryl's boss says, "I call Cheryl the queen of the flat–liners. No matter what is going on to the left or the right, she is extremely stable and always very careful about what she says."

Cafeteria manager Shirley Anthony handles federal applications for Free and Reduced Lunches at Franklinton Elementary. The application forms are confidential. Shirley says, "The parents are putting their business on that form. They are putting their jobs, the amount of money they make, their children's social security numbers on that form and putting it into my hands." Shirley honors the confidentiality of the information not only because her job requires it, but because she respects the families and the trust they have placed in her.

Custodian Carmen Duran sometimes assists the school staff with translating for Spanish–speaking families at school conferences. These conferences might involve classroom information or disciplinary issues. Barb Hastings, the ESL teacher, needed to meet with a family from Mexico whose dialect was unfamiliar to her. "I called Carmen in to be sure that I understood everything, because sometimes one word can change the meaning. Carmen is trustworthy. He does not talk to neighbors about school issues, and nothing goes beyond the walls in our conferences."

Circumstantial Evidence

Gossip needn't be false to be evil — there's a lot of truth that shouldn't be passed around.
—Frank A. Clark

Secretary Debbie Malsack offers another perspective on confidentiality. She contends that hearsay, or unofficial information, can cause others to become prejudiced. "Sometimes a child comes to our school with an informal record of poor behavior," she says. "If this is not shared with the staff, the child has the opportunity for a fresh start and may do amazingly well."

Debbie feels the same principle applies to adults. Over the years she knew employees who transferred to different schools due to conflicts. Sometimes the change of environment helped to resolve the issues. If the new staff had knowledge of the previous situation, they might have been less willing to give the employee a chance.

Debbie reminds us that it is important to know who has a legal right to even informal student information. Sometimes she receives phone inquiries about students. "Unless the caller is listed on the student's emergency card, information cannot be shared. And unless I can verify that the person on the phone is indeed the one named on the card, I do not share the information."

Engaged Ambassadors Respect and Protect Confidentiality

In the reports of these outstanding support staff members, you will see the word *respect* used often. When we respect others, we value them and we are considerate of their feelings. When we respect others, we do not break confidentiality outside the school or engage in inappropriate conversations in the lounge.

Unspoken words rarely hurt people. Relaying information about students is not harmless gossip. First, no gossip is harmless. Second, breaking confidentiality within the school situation can also be grounds for legal action.

Engaged Ambassadors care about their students and their coworkers. They treat confidential information in the same manner that they would want such information handled if it was about their own family. Engaged Ambassadors "respect and protect" all information they have access to at work.

Disengaged Employees	Engaged Ambassadors
☒ Eagerly relate information they are privy to at school	☑ Respect students and staff members
☒ Disregard the legal or moral implications of sharing information	☑ Realize that gossip is harmful
☒ Use gossiping as a way of feeling important	☑ Understand the protections provided for students in FERPA
	☑ Have a personal code of ethics that protects information, even if there is no law, policy, or rule

CHAPTER FOURTEEN

FROM "OTHER" TO ENGAGED AMBASSADOR

You are not here merely to make a living. You are here in order to enable the world to live more amply, with greater vision, with a finer spirit of hope and achievement. You are here to enrich the world, and you impoverish yourself if you forget the errand.
— Woodrow Wilson

A man went on a cruise. After a day or two, he noticed that the ship's crew wore their identification badges even when they were not on duty. When he ran into a crew member onshore, he inquired about the practice. "Aren't you off duty? Why are you wearing your identification in port?"

"Even when I am off duty," the fellow said, "I am an ambassador for our ship. The badges help the passengers to recognize me if they need any assistance."

You probably do not need to wear your identification tag outside of school to be recognized as an employee of the school district. Wherever you shop, worship, or go for entertainment, you are an ambassador for the school. Your actions and your words reflect on your place of employment. Engaged Ambassadors build bridges of goodwill for their school system. They are confident in their abilities and seek to build up their places of employment.

Engaged Ambassadors from a Superintendent's View

The three great essentials to achieve anything worthwhile are, first, hard work; second, stick–to–itiveness; third, common sense.
— Thomas Edison

Robert Hirsch, superintendent of Ocean Springs School District (Mississippi), appreciates his support staff and knows that they are Engaged Ambassadors. He says, "I think there is a tendency for people to lose focus on the classified individuals. I take the stand that they allow us to maintain a fluid operation. Without the support staff, we simply do not operate—we do not function."

Mr. Hirsch believes that school is a people and service business. He says, "At every level, beginning with the classified right up through certified teachers to the superintendent, we have to remember that our profession is 90 percent about feelings and perceptions. No matter what type of job you do, we are dealing first with children, the most precious commodity that adults have."

Mr. Hirsch offers five ideas for being an Engaged Ambassador for your school district:

1. You must be competent.
2. You must be flexible.
3. You must be timely and reliable.
4. You must be committed to specific goals and objectives.
5. You must appreciate people.

Do these points sound familiar? They are universal habits for being an Engaged Ambassador, whether you work in Virginia, California, Mississippi, or anywhere else. Let's review Superintendent Hirsch's five ideas and see how they align with the concepts we've covered in the book.

Competency

Don't just learn the tricks of the trade. Learn the trade.
—James Bennis

In chapter one, we discussed the importance of being a professional, which includes job competency. A professional does not need a college degree. A professional seeks new knowledge to increase his competency.

Your competence and your attitude make you a professional member of the educational team. Cafeteria manager Shirley Anthony says, "God has each of us in a certain place for a certain reason. Not everyone goes to college, but we are still professionals."

HVAC mechanic Richard "Tuck" Tucker believes that if something is worth doing, it is worth doing right. He says, "It is a pet peeve of mine to go back and do something twice. I would rather take the time and put quality into any job and do it right the first time."

His boss, Randy Connatser, says, "Tuck is one of those good team players. He is not only willing, but he is knowledgeable and experienced enough to help out with all the trades."

Secretary Debbie Malsack says that support personnel can increase their competency by attending staff development training, taking classes independently, or just by watching others on the job. She says, "There is always a need for improvement, no matter how much knowledge you might have." Debbie is confident in her skills and knowledge, yet she is always ready to learn something new. She says, "I need updates regularly, just like a computer, to keep up with all the changes that occur." She feels that challenging ourselves to learn new things sometimes takes us out of our comfort zone, but is critical to continued growth as a professional.

Flexibility

Trim your sails according to the wind.
— Chinese proverb

High–rise buildings and bridges must have a certain amount of flexibility engineered into their designs to withstand the forces of earth tremors and wind. Being flexible is a sign of strength, not weakness. In a storm, the trees that bend with the wind are not uprooted as easily as the rigid ones. Flexibility was the trait that many support staff members mentioned as critical to positively dealing with change and interruptions.

On the job, Engaged Ambassadors are flexible. They prioritize tasks and weigh interruptions by importance and urgency. They take into consideration the needs of the team and are willing to work toward compromise.

Timely and Reliable

Everything comes too late for those who only wait.
— Elbert Hubbard

When you need something done right, whom do you ask? For me, it is someone I trust to get the job done. It is a person who has earned that confidence because he or she has been reliable. You are referred to as a "support person" because a lot of responsibility is resting on your shoulders. What adjectives would your team leader use to describe you? Would *timely* and *reliable* be on the list?

Committed to Goals and Objectives

I'd rather attempt to do something great and fail
than to attempt to do nothing and succeed.
—Robert Schuller

What do you really believe about your school or district mission? Has it moved from your head to your heart? Are you dedicated to the mission, or do you feel locked into a dead–end job?

A few years ago, I was speaking in Huntsville, Alabama, to a large group of employees from both the public and private sectors. As I was explaining the concept of alignment between one's personal mission statement and the organization's mission, one man was on the edge of his seat. During our next break, he asked me for a business card. I received a phone call from him a few months later and he said, "Sam, thanks for what you said about becoming an on–purpose person. Because of you I have quit my job."

"You did what?" I thought I might need to send him a check or something.

"Don't worry," he said, "I have a job now." Jeff Greenhill left his job as a chemical engineer for the Tennessee Valley Authority to be a groom on a thoroughbred horse farm in Louisville, Kentucky. He said, "I simply could not be the motivated professional you were challenging us to become in Huntsville because I was pursuing my pension instead of my passion."

Two years later, I received a picture in the mail from Mr. Greenhill with a note that said, "I wanted you to have a photo of my first victory as a thoroughbred trainer. Thanks for all your encouragement."

As the late George Burns was fond of saying, "I would rather fail at what I love than succeed at what I hate."

Are you passionate about your job? Even if you want to do something different five years from now, do you see your current job as part of the plan and therefore come to work passionate about the opportunity to serve others?

Appreciate People

You have not lived a perfect day unless you've done something for someone who will never be able to repay you.

—Ruth Smeltzer

Appreciating students, teammates, supervisors, families, community members, and yourself is crucial to being an Engaged Ambassador. A school is a "people business." Robert Hirsch says, "We are all aware of the jobs we are hired to do, but it takes a special mentality to realize that education is a people business. Our business is about feelings. This is true at every level, whether it's the parents, teachers, or kids we are dealing with."

People need to be appreciated. Team members must be supportive of one another. Everything we do as Engaged Ambassadors shows our respect for others.

The "Little Bit More" Mentality

When I was in school, my dad used to say, "Sam, with your grades you could not possibly be cheating." I want my five kids to excel beyond my own achievements, so when I met a man whose children made straight A's all through high school and college, I asked him to share his secret with me. Here is what he said:

When my children were in middle school, every week or so I would ask them what it took to get a C, a B, or an A.

"To get a C," they would say, "you have to show up and do the basic work. To get a B, you have to do the basic work and a little bit more. To get an A, you have to do the work, a little bit more, and then throw in some extra effort."

At that point, I would remind my children that over 80 percent of their efforts were expended just to get a C. Why not do the little bit more and get a B or an A?

My friend's philosophy is the essence of this book. The difference between ordinary and extraordinary is the little extra. You are already working hard serving others. Why not develop the "little bit more" mentality and serve with a signature style? You will provide more than service; you will create memories and leave a legacy. Go ahead — liberate greatness!

Section 7:

Hall of Engaged Ambassadors

You have been introduced to support staff members from across the country as they've shared their hearts, their opinions, and their practices from the field. I invite you to read more about these Engaged Ambassadors. I know you will be encouraged by their stories.

Engaged Ambassador:

Shirley Anthony
Cafeteria Manager
Franklinton Elementary School
Washington Parish
Louisiana

Shirley Anthony's melt–in–your–mouth yeast rolls are legendary, but her smile is the reason the children, staff, and community love Mrs. Shirley. Reading teacher Ella Rose Bickham says that Shirley's smile is the inspiration for all at Franklinton Elementary School.

Shirley says, "Everyone who comes into the cafeteria is bringing either a positive or a negative attitude. So I try to deal with everyone with a smile. You know, someone may have a problem that day, and my smile might be the thing that tells him or her everything is going to be okay. You don't know what is going on in the children's homes, or even in the teachers' homes."

True Partners

Shirley describes her school as a family that works well together. "It makes me feel good to be part of the school team. Our principal, Mrs. Mary Henderson, is one of the best! She includes the support staff in luncheons and other staff activities. Some people think because you work in the kitchen or are a janitor that you are not important. At Franklinton, we all feel like an important part of the educational team because we are included in these things. It is not what your job title is, but what you put into it that counts."

Once, a teacher asked Shirley to show her class how to make yeast rolls. Shirley says, "The children were amazed at the process. They couldn't believe that little pieces of dough could rise up and turn into light rolls."

"It's a two–way thing," she says. "I like to help the teachers with projects like that. We like to work together."

Shirley also knows that having enough to eat helps a child to learn. She says, "When you go in the classroom and your stomach is growling, you can't pay attention to the teacher. Your mind cannot get off eating. A nutritious meal goes a long way."

Shirley's cafeteria team works together too. She will quickly correct anyone who refers to the cafeteria as "hers."

"It is not my cafeteria. It is our cafeteria and that is what I tell the employees. I'll pull my rings off and roll my sleeves up to pinch rolls with them. I tell them not to get behind if I'm working on the computer and they need me. I tell them to ask me for help. That is where teamwork comes in. We all work together."

Ambassadors of Love

"The point I want to share with other support staff is that you've got to have a loving heart," Shirley says. "This business is not about the dollar, it is about the love you have for people." She adds, "You don't talk down on your school; you lift your school up. School is family."

Read more about Shirley Anthony in Chapters 12, 13, and 14.

Engaged Ambassador:

Sharlene Barrois
Attendance Secretary
Belle Chasse High School
Formerly of Buras High School
Plaquemines School District
Louisiana

"Sharlene Barrois lost everything, including her house and the school where she worked for over twenty years, to Hurricane Katrina," says assistant principal Jemi Carlone. What Sharlene did not lose was her caring spirit and concern for the students who also faced this disaster.

Overcoming Tragedy

Sharlene did not let tragedy keep her down. She was able to relocate to another community and school where many of the families from her old high school had relocated. At Belle Chasse High School, she is a familiar face and an encourager for her former students from Buras High.

As attendance secretary, Sharlene checks in tardy students. She says, "They are late for various reasons, but no matter what, I try to make the kids feel comfortable coming in here and not fuss at them. I treat them like I want to be treated. I try to understand them and have a good relationship with them. When kids come in late, they may be upset. I want to get them into a happy mood before they get to the classroom. I remind them to be cheerful with their teachers. I don't want them to cause problems. I treat them with respect and I get that respect back."

Engaged Ambassador in the Storm

Sharlene is a familiar face from Buras for the dislocated parents as well. She says, "I often see parents in the community. Sometimes running in the store for a loaf of bread can take an hour." Because she experienced the same devastation as many of the students and families, she is able to empathize with the special needs of the community. This puts her in a unique position as an Engaged Ambassador. Sharlene always has good things to say about her school and makes a point to share those positives with others. When the students and families see Sharlene's example of making the best of a bad situation, they are encouraged to do the same.

Read more about Sharlene Barrois in Chapter 12.

Engaged Ambassador:

Pauline Cowan
Pre–K Teaching Assistant
South Knox Elementary School
Knox County Public Schools
Tennessee

Pauline Cowan's retirement did not last long. After a thirty–year career as a corporate child–care director, she looked forward to time for her flower garden and church activities. Retirement was fine for a while, but Pauline's heart yearned to be back with young children. When she heard that the new public school program for at–risk preschoolers was looking for a teaching assistant, Pauline applied for the job. She was hired right away!

The first year of the program, Pauline was assigned to a class in an off–campus building that did not have the amenities of a school building—no custodian, no cafeteria, no office, and no office equipment. Pauline served meals every day, cleaned the classroom and bathrooms, and took out the trash.

Preschool specialist Carol Idol says, "Pauline was the teaching assistant, the custodian, the chief cook and bottle washer. She never complained that other class assignments were in real school buildings. Instead, she smiled every day and performed her duties to the highest level for her students and their families. Nothing mattered more to Pauline than the education of her students."

From a Fashion Model to a Role Model

Pauline's mother believed in her. Because of her mother's love and encouragement, Pauline overcame childhood self–consciousness about being much taller than the other kids. The physical trait that threatened her became the foundation of a teen career as a fashion model.

Pauline knows the power of someone believing in you. She is there for the children, and she takes special interest in those who might need extra encouragement. She says, "We had one little girl who had a hard time adjusting to school. I paired myself with her. For everything she was asked to do, I was there encouraging her. She was not even comfortable having her picture made with the class, so I sat in a chair next to the group and put her in my lap—with myself out of the picture. That was the first photo her mother had of her."

Pauline gave her own sons the gift of an adult believing in and encouraging them. She continues to give that gift to the youngsters in her life. Her concern for children provides a role model for those around her.

Pajama Model?

Pauline accompanies her current classroom teacher, Judith Hiscock, on home visits at the beginning of the school year. She willingly volunteers her time to participate in these visits because of her love for the children and her desire to ease the transition to the first day of school.

At the end of the year, Judith and Pauline make another home visit—but this one is in the evening, dressed in their pajamas. Why would a fashion model wear pajamas to visit a home? Because she loves to see the delight in each child's face when she and Judith arrive with a stack of bedtime books. Pauline and Judith tuck the child and siblings into bed, then read a bedtime story to them. A book of bedtime stories is left for the parent to continue the practice. Still modeling, aren't you, Pauline?

Read more about Pauline Cowan in Chapters 6, 7, 9, and 13.

Engaged Ambassador:

Delight Creech
Communities in Schools Director
Hudson Area Schools
Michigan

Delight Creech is the Communities in Schools Director for her district, so she functions as a highly visible Engaged Ambassador. Her superintendent, Kathy Malnar, says that Delight goes beyond expectations to address the needs of the children and families in the district.

Bridge Over Troubled Waters

Lori Lancaster, assistant to the superintendent, works closely with Delight. She says, "Delight is our liaison to the homeless and works with families in crisis. She sees all kinds of trauma, but she never comes to work in a bad mood. She is always upbeat and happy, concerned about everybody else. She has a way of dealing with tragedy in a positive way. She always wants to know what she can do to help. Delight is there for the families and students, and she is there for the school staff."

Equipping for Success

Delight's district uses a formal program called, *40 Proven Assets* (Search Institute, Minneapolis, MN), to equip their students for success. One of the premises of the program is that youth need support from at least three caring and supportive adults, in addition to their parents.

As Engaged Ambassadors in the schools, support persons touch lives every day. Delight shares some informal ways you can make a difference in the life of a child, even if your district does not have a formal program.

First, Delight says that all school employees are ambassadors, but that bus drivers are "bookends." They are the staff members who make the first and last impressions of the day on students. If you are a bookend, you not only touch the lives of the riders, you also demonstrate your professionalism and pride in the courtesy you show to other drivers along your route.

"It is the little things that matter," Delight says. "Support persons see the students every day. They can walk through the lunchroom and say hello, and call a student by name. That is being a caring adult in the child's life. That is building a relationship."

Delight knows that when you acknowledge a person's presence by smiling or offering a word of encouragement, you are an Engaged Ambassador.

Read more about Delight Creech in Chapter 11.

Engaged Ambassador:

Barry Crocker
Head Custodian
Nicholson Elementary School
Cobb County Schools
Georgia

Barry Crocker is proud of his work at Nicholson Elementary School. "I look at it like this," Barry says. "It's all in how you view your contribution and how you view yourself. I tell people, 'You get what you put into your work.' If I do my personal best, it shows. That's what I want to reflect to the students. And I get a positive return on it."

Visible Member of the Educational Team

Barry mentors and encourages students at Nicholson. He says, "I go down to the special needs kindergarten class and sit for fifteen to twenty minutes doing centers with the children several mornings a week." Interactions such as this make Barry a more visible part of the educational team.

Assistant principal Cheryl Mauldin says, "Barry believes in the kids and the parents, and they know that. Our school outperforms other schools with similar populations because our kids believe that they can succeed, and they do. This confidence comes from encouragers like Barry."

Guidance counselor Becky Grindstaff also feels Barry makes a difference. "We have a very transient student population, with 30 percent of the students on free or reduced lunches," she says. "Barry keeps the buildings and grounds clean. Sometimes the children do not have clean areas like this at home. Barry is a positive male figure, and many of our students do not have that at home."

Good Communication: Key to Mutual Respect

The curse of many custodians is bathroom graffiti. But not at Nicholson Elementary. Barry does several things to cultivate a relationship of mutual respect among the custodial staff and others in the school, and it all begins with good communication.

He attends student council meetings and works with the students to solve such problems as bathroom mischief. One solution was to have the students create posters for the bathrooms encouraging pride in a clean facility. Barry says, "We all work here, we all live here. We need to work together to keep the school clean for hygiene and for safety." He chuckles and says, "If there is an occasional problem, the kids are quick to report the culprit. Having a good relationship with the students is the biggest help in gaining their respect."

Barry is a member of the Building Leadership Team, which includes the administrators, counselor, and grade–level team leaders. "I can always talk to them about what my staff is trying to do to make the school a safer, cleaner place for everyone." Barry also keeps open communication with the PTA and the Nicholson Foundation members. "Keeping the school clean and safe is a community–wide effort."

Dealing with Frustrations

Frustrations and conflicts occur in every school. When a teacher or a student has been inconsiderate, or he is just having a bad day Barry goes to the office and vents his frustrations behind closed doors.

"I sit in Ms. Mauldin's rocking chair. I rock that thing about ninety miles per hour, and I tell her about what has upset me. She gives me time to calm down, and then we look at the overall picture."

Barry does not carry his frustrations on his sleeve. "When I walk out of that office, I'm okay. I'm smiling. I don't let stuff affect me. I don't take it home with me. When it's done, it's done. If the situation is something I can't change, I accept that. I move on and don't hold a grudge."

"I've come to realize that I can't change everything or have everything my way all the time. I've learned to let it go and let things go. I take each day and do the best I can. I stay as positive as I can. When I reflect a positive outlook, that's what I get back."

Read more about Barry Crocker in Chapters 3, 9, and 11.

Engaged Ambassador:

Sherry Cunningham
Educational Assistant and Bus Driver
Unity School
Lincoln County Schools
Tennessee

"We may never know what influence we have in the lives of the children," says Sherry Cunningham, "but they should always know that we care about them and love them. They are important and should feel that way every day at school."

Sherry applied for a bus–driver position six years ago after realizing that the children with disabilities that she worked with needed consistency throughout the day.

"I felt it was important to become a bus driver so that I was not only working with the children in school, but I could also be the smiling face they saw when they got on the bus in the mornings, and got off the bus in the afternoon."

Early–Morning Sunshine

Sherry's cheery disposition brightens the early–morning ride for the youngsters and eases their transition into the classroom. She has the opportunity to see and speak to the parents when the children board the bus, and often learns if a child has had a rough morning at home. Since Sherry is the special–needs assistant for the children she transports, she is able to share this information with the teacher.

Schoolboard member Brenda Ables says, "Sherry is concerned for the students she serves. She makes sure that they have the care they need from the time they leave home until they return. Above all, Sherry loves the kids."

Lifelong Learner

Sherry believes that learning never stops. When she had students who used sign language, she enrolled in a sign–language class. She says, "As support persons, we should educate ourselves to better serve our students and teachers."

Sherry's state is one of many that now require teaching assistants to take the ParaPro test. Sherry was the first in her district to take the examination, and she encouraged and helped others prepare for it as well.

She says, "Passing the ParaPro Assessment (www.ets.org) signifies that we are Highly Qualified paraprofessionals, not just aides or helpers in the classroom. We can have a title—we are important. I take this very seriously and want to be the best I can be at what I do. Our children are our future and we must be there to teach and influence their lives in a positive way."

Member of a Professional Organization

Sherry is active in the National Educational Association and serves as the treasurer for her local group. She feels that it is important to be involved in a professional organization that can provide information and support.

Proud to be an Engaged Ambassador

Sherry is an Engaged Ambassador for Unity School. She loves her school and wants everyone to know it! She says, "My school is my second home and I love to be there. I am proud of my school. It is a caring place, and that caring goes out into the community. I refer to Unity as 'my' school, because that is the way I feel."

Read more about Sherry Cunningham in Chapters 5 and 13.

Engaged Ambassador:

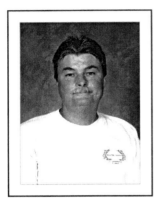

John Dorman
Custodian
Griffin Elementary School
Broward County
Florida

John Dorman is the lead custodian at Griffin Elementary School. He says, "I am proud of my school. Every visitor leaves this school with a good experience. Griffin Elementary is a special place."

Understanding the Feelings of Students

John knows that students sometimes say things that can hurt the feelings of their classmates. Not only does John comfort a student who does not make it to the restroom before vomiting, he also talks to the other students about not teasing the child. "I talk to the kids to get them to walk in the sick child's shoes. When I do this, they don't ridicule the child who got sick in the hallway or classroom."

A Welcoming Place for Learning

John works as a team with his custodial crew to make Griffin Elementary a welcoming place for learning. "Students are going to do better, regardless of what they are learning, if they have a clean place and a clean atmosphere. The kids come first. I try to always put kids and teachers before myself."

The Power of Putting Ideas Together

John says, "We don't have too many problems here, but if there is one, we sit down and discuss it. I like to get everyone's input. I believe two heads are better than one. When you put ideas together, there are many times when someone has a better way to do something. Even though I've been doing this job longer than the others on my crew, they may see things in a little bit different light."

John chuckles and continues, "Many times I say that we need to do something in a certain way. Then someone comes up and suggests starting in the middle. I'm up for healthy criticism any day of the week. If someone has a better idea, I'm ready to listen."

The Challenge of Conflict

If team members have a disagreement with each other, John takes the stance of mediator and encourages them to talk about their differences of opinion and work out a resolution. If John is unable to help his crew work things out, he knows where to go for assistance. He says, "Conflict resolution is not one of my strong points, but we have an assistant principal and principal who are very gifted in that area. When I feel that I can't handle something, I take it to the next step of going to the assistant principal or principal." John has probably picked up some great tips for dealing with conflict by watching how his administrators handle situations.

Engaged Ambassador

John loves the kids and their families. "When I run into them at the gas station, it is like we are family. We exchange pleasantries: 'How are you doing? What's coming up at the school?'"

John enjoys working with the PTA on after–school activities. "I try to put my services out there for them. I remind them to get with me so we can get a list going of the things they will need for the event. I don't want to get caught up at the last minute trying to get everything in line. When we work together ahead of time, everything goes smoothly."

Being an Engaged Ambassador is what John strives for. "I try to treat people like I want to be treated, and I treat the school like it is my home. I spend about as much time here as I do at home. I have been here for twenty–four years, and this is home. I never hesitate to tell people that."

John adds, "The lady I work for is absolutely wonderful. She has great faith in us, and we try not to let her down."

Read more about John Dorman in Chapters 3, 9, and 11.

Engaged Ambassador:

Carmen Duran
Building Superintendent
Northside Elementary
Elko County School District
Nevada

Carmen Duran heads the custodial team at Northside Elementary as well as being responsible for overseeing the building at Ruby Valley, a two–room school sixty miles north of his base school.

Principal Kevin Melcher says, "Carmen is a leader. His success in supervising three other custodians is because he rolls up his sleeves and works with them. His staff respects him because he respects them."

Assisting Hispanic Parents

Barbara Hastings teaches English as a Second Language classes at Northside. She thinks Carmen goes beyond the call of duty when needed to interpret for non–English–speaking families.

"Lots of times the parents come to me to ask questions about the school because they know me," Carmen says. "Early in the morning, I may be the only one here who speaks Spanish. Even if a new family does not know me yet, they talk and we become friends. They say I am like a friend. I want them to feel at home at the school."

Once, Carmen was asked to interpret for parents at a disciplinary meeting about their child. They arrived early, so he introduced himself and helped them feel a little more comfortable in a situation that was tense for them.

Carmen's willingness to assist provides a bridge between the school and the families, and helps them understand that the school is there to support them.

Friendly and Nice

Carmen is an Engaged Ambassador with all the families, no matter what language they speak. He says, "I try to be friendly and nice, even if I don't know the parents. I always greet people when they come to the school. That way the parents are comfortable bringing the kids to the school, and the kids are happy to be here."

Read more about Carmen Duran in Chapters 11 and 13.

Engaged Ambassador:

Marcia Forsythe
Kindergarten Assistant and Lunchroom Monitor
Kemptown Elementary School
Frederick County
Maryland

Ask anyone at Kemptown Elementary School about Marcia Forsythe, and her ready smile will be one of the first things mentioned!

Principal Steve Parsons says, "Marcia brings skills, enthusiasm, and understanding of little ones to her position as an instructional assistant and lunchroom monitor."

A Talented Multitasker

Marcia seamlessly manages several responsibilities. She is the roving kindergarten assistant and cafeteria monitor, and handles car duty at dismissal time. Marcia is also in charge of ordering all the teaching supplies for her school. She assists with classroom coverage when needed, and she runs copies and does other clerical work in the office.

Marcia says that her kindergarten–assistant position is her primary job assignment, so that is her priority. But even that is a juggle, she rotates among several half–day kindergarten classrooms. Her early–morning responsibilities include helping in the office, but as soon as the students arrive, she stops by the classrooms to greet them, then returns to her clerical work.

Member of the Educational Team

In the classroom, Marcia does centers with the students. These include instruction in phonics, writing, and word study. Her team plans by the month, so Marcia has the center plans several weeks early. She says, "I get my instructional materials ready, and I tweak the plans for the different learning levels."

Assistant principal Catherine Poling describes Marcia as a critical team member who could run a classroom well on her own.

The teachers value Marcia's insights and input into the planning for instruction. Marcia says, "Before I started the kindergarten job, I didn't feel like part of the team, but being included in the planning makes me feel like I belong."

Laughing Lunch Lady and Cheerleader

As soon as the morning kindergartners leave, Marcia hurries to the lunchroom for her monitor duties. "I can't be late," she says, "because the teachers only have a short time for their own lunch break." Marcia loves the students and feels that lunchtime should be a pleasant time for social interaction. She ends the lunch period with "joke time," allowing her little stand–up comics to share the latest riddles and funny stories.

Marcia describes herself as a cheerleader. "I can only say good things about Kemptown. It is a unique school and a wonderful place to work. It is easy to be an Engaged Ambassador when you are working with such a good team."

Read more about Marcia Forsythe in Chapters 3 and 13.

Engaged Ambassador:

Coleen Humberson
Cafeteria Manager
Word of God Catholic School
Woodland Hills School District
Pennsylvania

Coleen Humberson does not like "three strikes and you are out." She says, "Some cafeterias have a three–strike policy where you are given a peanut–butter–and–jelly sandwich the third time you forget your lunch money. I refuse to do that. I don't want the children to be upset and it is not really their responsibility. Instead, I make a reminder phone call to the parents."

One of Coleen's own children forgot his lunch money in elementary school and was embarrassed when he was given a sandwich. "It upset me when my child was treated that way, so I would never do the same to another child. The cafeteria should be a place to relax, not a place where a child is a nervous wreck over forgotten lunch money."

Polling Place

When a new menu item is served, Coleen takes a student poll. The children feel empowered when they have a voice in which items they would like to see stay on the menu. Coleen says, "There used to be menu items that the kids disliked and would not eat. We cook what they like and still provide healthy meals. This has made lunchtime more enjoyable for the children."

Partnering with the Classroom

Coleen's school houses classes for special–needs students. Part of their curriculum includes life skills for employment and independent living. "We have three students this year who are working with us. They come down and help us get set up for lunch. We teach them skills like putting out the condiments, washing the tables, and coding the cans to go on the shelves."

Coleen's school also has a student interaction program with

the nearby Pittsburg School for the Deaf. Each school year, several of the hearing–impaired high–school students assist at Word of God School for several hours a day, and one works in the cafeteria. Coleen says, "The student we have this year makes our salad dressings and prepares the cheese cups. Our classes of hearing students go to the school for the deaf and learn silk–screening, sewing, and many other things. All the hearing children and teachers in our school have learned sign language."

When Coleen was in elementary school, there were no special–needs students at Word of God Catholic School. (Yes, cafeteria manager Coleen Humberson and her own children all attended the school where she now works.) She is thrilled to have the special–needs programs there now. "It is so helpful. When I was young we did not interact with any children with special needs. I watch the kids now, and they are so good with one another."

Taking Initiative

Maggie Sabol's children attend Coleen's school. Maggie says, "Coleen is devoted to the educational success of each child in the school, even though her own children are grown. She deserves a commendation for all of her efforts throughout the year. Not only did she hold her own salary back for several months while getting the lunch program started, she also held a spaghetti dinner fund–raiser to purchase a new stove for the kitchen."

With Coleen in the kitchen, Maggie says, "At Word of God Catholic School, it's not just *no child left behind*, it's *no child left hungry*."

Read more about Coleen Humberson in Chapter 9.

Engaged Ambassador:

Cheryl Jalanivich
Secretary to the Superintendent of Schools
Ocean Springs School District
Mississippi

Cheryl Jalanivich is the secretary to superintendent Robert Hirsch. You might think that a central office secretary in that position would have little contact with the classroom.

"Everything that I do ultimately impacts the children," Cheryl says. "I may be supporting administrators who support the teachers, or I may be directly supporting the teachers in some manner. But it all flows down to the children." Since Mr. Hirsch became superintendent, Cheryl has had the opportunity to spend some time in the classroom. She regularly visits the schools, where she may read to students or assist the teacher with a lesson.

A True Professional

Cheryl's boss describes her as extremely competent and experienced. Mr. Hirsch says, "She has developed a huge knowledge base over the years. If she does not know something, she will track down the information to serve the person who needs it. It does not matter whether that person is another employee, a parent, a student, or a member of the community. She is always helpful in that way. She appreciates all people, beginning with her family, her coworkers, and her friends."

Cheryl's dream was to be a teacher. Circumstances kept her from going to college, but she sent three daughters, and all three are teachers now. Even without her teaching degree, Cheryl followed her heart and built a career in the educational field as a support person. She is a true professional in her area—so much so that she currently serves as state president of the Secretarial and Board Clerk division of the Mississippi School Board Association.

Read more about Cheryl Jalanivich in Chapters 8, 9, and 13.

Engaged Ambassador:

Joanne Jones
School Nurse
Woestina Elementary School
Schalmont Central School District
New York

Joanne Jones has worked at Woestina Elementary for twenty–one years, and she attended elementary school there herself.

Board member Sandra Beloncik says, "Joanne is highly regarded inside and outside of the school. She is always aware of family situations and offers support and guidance when it is needed."

Classroom Involvement

Joanne likes to be involved in the classrooms and often helps with student projects and trips. She worked with the PTO and teachers to stop the spread of contagious illnesses by instigating a war against germs in the classroom. Students are eager members of the "Clean–Up Club" and clean their desktops with premoistened antibacterial wipes at the end of each day. This simple step has decreased the absentee rate considerably at Woestina Elementary.

Relating to the Community

Joanne feels that being a part of the community for so long helps her to be an Engaged Ambassador for the school. "Because I know and relate to the community so well," she says, "I can help things go smoothly at school. I not only know the students, I know most of their parents and grandparents too.

Read more about Joanne Jones in Chapters 3 and 13.

Engaged Ambassador:

Joan Kellner
Head Secretary
C. G. Stangel Elementary School
Manitowoc Public Schools
Wisconsin

"Joan is a shining star and a joy to be around. Her work is done efficiently, timely, and without complaint," says her principal, Debby Shimanek. "She is exceptional in her willingness to serve the families and students beyond what is expected."

Positively a People Person

Joan loves working with people, including students, parents, staff, and the community. She stops whatever project she is involved in when someone comes into the office or the phone rings. "People are the most important part of my job and they come first."

When upset parents come into the office, Joan responds in kindness and listens to their concerns. Once, a father phoned the school to apologize to her. He had lost his temper in the office earlier that day. Joan says, "I never judge a person. There are always two sides to a disagreement. I just listened to the father and did not make comments when he was upset. If I had reacted negatively to his raised voice, I don't think he would have called and apologized."

Taking the Initiative

Joan started two special projects at Stangel. One is a hallway bulletin board, which features newspaper articles about staff members, students, and their families. She says, "I asked our awesome PTO to purchase a laminator for me. I place the laminated articles on a bulletin board for visitors to our school to view. When I take the photos down, I send them home for the student or staff member to keep. This has generated many positive comments. The families are thrilled to have a copy that will last forever.

Joan's second project is a two–part frame in a main hallway. The top frame says, "Our Stangel First Graders Have Grown into

Stangel Sixth Graders." The bottom frame contains first–grade photos of the current sixth graders. Since Joan does not want to leave anyone out, she also includes first–grade photos of those students who did not attend the school in first grade. Joan enjoys doing "a little bit more" to make all students feel important at C. G. Stangel Elementary School.

Read more about Joan Kellner in Chapters 9, 11, 12, and 13.

Engaged Ambassador:

Debbie Malsack
Secretary
Durkee Elementary School
Kenosha Unified School District No. 1
Wisconsin

Debbie Malsack feels that the secretary is a crucial Engaged Ambassador in the school. "Parents want to leave their most precious commodity, their children, in good hands. By being gracious, courteous, and helpful, you solidify the impression that they are important to you and the school." Her motto is to *saturate everyone with kindness.*

Engaging Parents and Coworkers

Sometimes upset parents will come into the office and voice their frustrations to Debbie. She says, "I never take irate or upset people personally. I just listen. Anyone who is listened to, and treated kindly, will feel validated and will calm down. I then offer any services that are in my realm. By showing this courtesy, I soon develop a rapport with parents."

Debbie says that it is critical to be a good role model for newer office staff. "When those around me see how I deal with parents in an empathetic way, they begin to respond the same way. I explain to them that these parents may have situations that we are not aware of. How we treat them can either be the straw that breaks the camel's back or the ray of light for that day."

Impacting the Entire School

Debbie says that the climate of the entire school can be more positive when the office is a warm and welcoming environment. She feels this happens when the staff assumes an "attitude of gratitude" philosophy, when they remember not to take situations personally, and when they are empathetic and helpful.

Inviting Community Volunteers

Debbie coordinates a mentoring program with a local business and the local Jewish literacy program. These mentors are not parents, and after the first year of the program, several nearly dropped out. Debbie discovered that they did not feel appreciated and did not feel they had made a difference with the children. Debbie took the concerns seriously and created a plan to match mentors and students more closely. The "little bit more" attitude that she invested in solving the problem rather than ignoring it saved the mentorship program. For the past ten years, the same mentors have remained in the program.

Debbie personally greets the mentors when they enter the building. Once a year, the school purchases small tokens of appreciation and the children decorate special gift bags. The children love giving the gifts and the mentors love receiving them, especially with the personalized wrapping.

Making the School Family Friendly

Debbie tries to accommodate parents whenever possible. She noticed that parents often brought preschool siblings when they came to the school to take care of business or attend a parent conference. So she offers books, paper, and crayons to occupy the youngsters while the parents complete forms or speak with a teacher. When these preschoolers are old enough to come to kindergarten, they will already have a positive feeling about the school.

If a parent with younger children comes to pick up a sick student, Debbie escorts the ill child to the car and takes the sign–out book to the car. This little act of kindness keeps the parent from having to bundle the babies into the building.

Note: Debbie Malsack attended Sam's Sizzling Customer Service for Schools in her school district in 2007. At the break, she spoke with him and expressed her appreciation for including support staff in the seminar. Her enthusiasm was one of the inspirations for writing a book specifically for school support staff. We approached her with ideas as the book was formulating and appreciate the feedback she provided us. Thanks, Debbie!

Read more about Debbie Malsack in Chapters 13 and 14.

Engaged Ambassador:

Jim Murley
Bus Driver and Founder of Reading
Riders Program
Waxahachie ISD
Texas

Jim Murley wanted a change. He had
been an auto–parts sales representative
for seventeen years. "I told my wife that I
needed to do something different with my
life," he says. "I had originally desired to
be a teacher, so I got my first job with the school system as a special–
needs assistant. I felt a real compassion for the kids."

Taking Compassion to the Road

After a few years, Jim left the assistant position to become a
bus driver. His supervisor, Gary Coffey, is glad to have Jim as part
of the transportation team. Jim drives several routes, which include
elementary students, secondary students, and students attending the
English as a Second Language program.

Still Teaching

Gary says that Jim is a positive role model for students on
his bus and takes a personal interest in each of them. He cheerfully
greets them by name and asks how they are doing. If he knows certain
students had a Little League game the evening before, he will inquire
about that. If he knows someone is working on a project for school,
he may ask how it is coming. Jim knows his students. He even took
a Spanish class so he could greet his Hispanic students and their
parents.

A few years ago, Jim wanted to do more to encourage his kids.
"Instead of another year of them picking on one another, I wanted to
try something new," he says. "I wanted to give them something to
focus on, something that would keep them calm on the bus."

Jim decided that reading on the bus would be the perfect
solution, especially for his elementary run. If he could get the kids to
join in, they would stop picking on one another, have extra practice

reading, and get some of their homework done before getting home, and Jim would be able to focus more on driving and less on student squabbles. Jim's plan started small, but within a couple of years, the whole school system knew about Jim Murley's Reading Rider Program, and other drivers in the district began the program on their buses.

Teachers noticed that the reluctant readers in the classroom were making gains in their reading assessments and they were reading for pleasure. Several children who did not like to read began eagerly participating in the classroom Accelerated Reading Program. The children noticed the difference and excitedly told Mr. Jim about their improved grades.

It Is Never Too Late to Follow a Dream

Jim Murley is the father of four adult children and grandfather of four grandchildren, but he recently took the first step toward his dream of being a teacher. He enrolled in college and is taking classes scheduled around his bus runs. Jim has goals and specific objectives to complete his sociology degree and become a school counselor. Way to go, Mr. Jim!

Read more about Jim Murley in Chapters 5 and 12.

Engaged Ambassador:

Telice Ostrinski
Secretary
Student Assistance Program/Family
Resource Center
San Bernardino City USD
California

"I think all front–desk persons should portray an image of professionalism," says Telice Ostrinski. "I take pride in making sure I have a good attitude when I come to work. I come to do a job and I need to do it the best I can with a smile on my face. I want the parents to feel comfortable when they are seeking information or assistance for their children."

Telice's former supervisor, Karen Wilson, oversaw fifteen assistance programs and more than fifty staff members, with Telice as her only clerical support. Karen says, "We were partners, equals, and friends, even though our job titles said otherwise. I always told Telice that the only thing that made us different was that I had a piece of paper—my degree. She could do anything that I did in the job."

Lifetime Learner

Telice took every opportunity to learn new skills and acquire more information on the job, but her dream has always been to go to college. She recently took the step to follow her dream and began taking college courses part time.

"I am back in school and eventually I will get that piece of paper," she says. "Right now I'm doing one class at a time, but next semester I will do two at a time. I am getting the general–education classes out of the way by doing them online. That has been easier than going to a classroom because of my obligations to my family."

Telice has three children—the oldest is also starting college in the fall—and family comes first. "It is very important to me to be available for them when I need to be. My husband is a fireman and may be away from home for days when he is working a fire."

Telice feels it is important to be a lifetime learner. She says, "I will have more to offer if I continue my education and become more informed. On the job, I learned everything I could about counseling, and that is what I am working toward now. I want to get my degree to be a counselor."

Valuing Yourself

Taking classes is something that Telice is doing for herself. She continues to devote her life to her family and her job, but going to college is a fulfillment of a dream that she put on hold for many years.

"I think it is important to value yourself as well. When you know you are doing something for yourself—to improve your personality or advance your career—you feel better about yourself. And I think when you feel better about yourself, you are able to offer more to others."

Advice for Going Back to School

With three kids, a firefighter husband, and a demanding job, it would have been easy for Telice to give up on her dream of going to college. She has advice for other support personnel who are considering more education but think that their lives are too busy. She says, "Bite the bullet. Stop procrastinating and just do it!"

The greatest journey always begins with one small step.

Read more about Telice Ostrinski in Chapters 3 and 9.

Engaged Ambassador:

Melody Sankey
Secretary
Newcastle Middle School
Weston County School District #1
Wyoming

"Melody Sankey loves kids," says her principal, Scott Shoop. "Whether she is applying a bandage, keeping score at a varsity basketball game, or delivering a message, she is friendly and supportive. The students love her, and that makes an impact on the Newcastle Middle School community."

Melody's personal goal is to always do her best and make people feel welcome at Newcastle. She must be succeeding, because visitors to the school consistently comment on her friendliness and the outstanding job she does as the middle school's "first impression."

Not So Invincible

Middle–school students have the reputation of being invincible, but Melody knows that they are vulnerable and need encouragement from the adults in their environment. When they come into the office, she takes time to visit with each one. "I can tell when the kids are having a bad day and need a shoulder or a hug," she says. "It's easy to read their body language and know when they need more than they are saying. In this job, you have to be a compassionate person. Every kid has positives, and they sometimes need someone to find those positives and point them out."

Sharing Knowledge

Melody is known as the "go to" person for help with the countywide student–management software. She turned down a position at the district office in that capacity because she did not want to leave the kids. Instead, she offered to mentor other secretaries while maintaining her job at Newcastle.

Melody says that there is always something new to learn, and she takes every opportunity to continue her education. She is excited to attend the Wyoming School Secretaries conference each year, held in conjunction with the Elementary and Secondary Principals Association convention.

Making a Difference

Melody's ability to treat everyone with warmth makes her an Engaged Ambassador for the entire school community. Melody believes that finding ways to help staff, students, and visitors is an important part of her job. "Just letting them know that they have someone to talk to can make all the difference. This helps to create a sense of camaraderie within the building and a safe environment for students."

Melody's greatest reward comes from the kids. "I receive letters from former students, thanking me for showing that I cared about them. Or they tell me how I made a difference in their lives. That, to me, is the gratification of the job."

Read more about Melody Sankey in Chapters 6, 9, 11, and 13.

Engaged Ambassador:

Belva Sarten
School Health Aide
Wyandotte Avenue Elementary
Oroville City ESD
California

Belva Sarten is on the road most of the day. In addition to being the part–time health aide in four schools, she serves seven additional schools, monitoring for head lice and educating parents in how to deal with the problem. Before Belva came on the job, her county had a high absentee rate due to lice. Parents would treat their children and send them back to school. But within a few days, they would have lice again and miss more school. Belva's work includes parental education on treating the home as well as the head. She even goes into the homes and helps the parents with the eradication procedures.

Bridging the Gap

Belva has a great sense of humor about her job, but at the same time, she is compassionate. She understands the embarrassment a student and family feel when they have lice. She respects her students and their families. She says, "I never look down on anyone because of their circumstances."

Belva is an Engaged Ambassador who bridges the gap between school and community daily. Since she works in the homes with parents, they often seek her advice for other family issues. She says, "I am a good listener. I never interrupt when the parents are talking to me. If they ask my advice about a situation, I refer them to the appropriate agency or person."

She also works as the liaison with the police department's "Shoe to Fit" program. This program provides new shoes for needy children. Belva first gets permission from the parents to order shoes for their children. After the order is placed, a police officer delivers the shoes to the school. Belva says, "I bring the children to my office individually, and they get new shoes and six new pairs of socks from the police officer. Some children are afraid of the police, and this helps them to see the officer as a friend."

Teaming with the School Board

When Belva realized that many homes did not have soap and shampoo, she approached the school board and asked if they would consider donating unused travel toiletries from their vacations and business trips. After hearing about this effort, many community members began sending travel toiletries to Belva. Now, when Belva visits a home, she is able to leave supplies for the children and families.

Standing a Little Taller

School board member Kathy White says that Belva is an inspiration. Her love for the students has done more than improve their attendance. She likes the way Belva describes it: "When you are clean, have new shoes and nice clothes, and when you don't have to worry about lice, you stand a little taller. Your confidence level goes up."

Read more about Belva Sarten in Chapter 13.

Engaged Ambassador:

Keith Seifert
Facilities Supervisor
North Penn High School
North Penn School District
Pennsylvania

Fire drill! Keith Seifert's 530,000–square–foot facility, housing more than four thousand students and staff, is evacuated seamlessly in less than five minutes. Keith, who is also a volunteer firefighter, says that school safety is a priority, especially with such a large campus. "If there is a safety concern or something is not quite up to code," he says, "I will notice it and take care of it. We hope that fire or other emergencies do not happen to us, but the possibility is always there, so we constantly work to provide a safe environment for our students and staff."

Building Use is a Bridge to the Community

Linda Abram, Parent and Community Involvement Specialist for North Penn, says, "Keith approaches challenges that others would be daunted by, and he inspires coworkers to rally alongside him in much the same way. He has been instrumental in perfecting our graduation for more than one thousand students, and he takes care of the details for regular, extracurricular, and community use of the facility."

Keith does not like the limelight and sees himself as a behind–the–scenes ambassador. Linda says, "He may not think he is on the forefront, but everyone in the community and school knows that Keith is the one orchestrating what goes on in this building. Even if you do not see him, he is running around to ensure that everything is done to support the activity. Keith does not need strokes, accolades, or recognition, but his leadership and organizational skills are known and appreciated."

Recognition for "Behind the Scenes" Excellence

Keith is proof that excellence—even behind the scenes—is

noticed. Recently, he was named to the Superintendent's Honor Roll. This recognition goes to one certified staff member and one support staff member each year. Part of the award was a monetary gift, which had to be used within the school. Keith felt that he received the recognition only because of the support of those twenty–nine men and women who work for him, and he wanted to share the honor with his team.

"I used some of the money to have a picnic for my custodial staff," he says. "After graduation and before we started the summer cleaning, we took an afternoon and enjoyed hamburgers and hot dogs. That was a break from their usual work and a way for me to thank them."

Engaged Ambassadors like Keith appreciate and acknowledge the support they receive from their team members. They realize that success is a team accomplishment, not an individual triumph.

Read more about Keith Seifert in Chapter 9.

Engaged Ambassador:

Stephanie Townsend
Bus Driver
Amelia County Public Schools
Virginia

Bus drivers are the first and the last school employees to have contact with the students each day. Because of that, Stephanie Townsend says that her words and attitude play a part in getting the kids off to a positive start for the day, and in helping to calm any who had a rough day before they get off the bus in the afternoon.

She says, "In the mornings the students are just getting out of bed, and some even bring their breakfast onto the bus. So the mornings are normally quiet. By the afternoon things are a little more wide open." Stephanie does not mind the noise and says that the students on her bus are great. She understands that they have been in classes for six hours and need time to unwind with their friends. When Stephanie's students are unloading at school in the mornings, she sends each off with encouragement for the day. She cares about their upcoming tests and assignments, and is always willing to listen to their concerns.

Second Mom

Stephanie transports all ages on her bus route, from preschoolers to high schoolers. "I love my kids. It is a big age range, but my high–school students help with my younger ones. Some of the little guys are on the bus for an hour, and the older students will read to them."

"After driving the same students for several years, you really get to know them and watch them grow up. I call them my kids, and I feel like I am a second mom to some of them. I treat them all with respect and they respect me."

Read more about Stephanie Townsend in Chapters 6 and 13.

Engaged Ambassador:

Richard "Tuck" Tucker
HVAC Mechanic
Maintenance Department
Frederick County Public Schools
Maryland

Tuck Tucker loves his job. "I've been crawling inside boilers since I was fourteen years old," he says. "My father had a heating and air–conditioning business, and I worked for him for many years. I was twenty–nine years old when I started with the school board, and I've been here for twenty–nine years."

Tuck's supervisor, Randy Connatser, describes Tuck as a specialist in his area and a team player who is a definite benefit to the maintenance department.

The Frederick County Director of Maintenance and Operations, Robert Wilkinson, also has praise and respect for Tuck's abilities and his work ethic. He says, "Tuck is the person we call when we have an emergency and are faced with having to close a facility if the heating system cannot be rendered operational. Despite his high level of skill and expertise, he is just as likely to be found crawling inside a boiler to perform maintenance or rebuild a section. He is a no–nonsense, hard–working individual. More importantly, he is a genuine pleasure to be around."

Tuck chuckles when asked if he still crawls into boilers. "Yes, but with age comes a few extra pounds, and I have to squeeze real hard to get in sometimes. My partner, Steve Frush, teases that we are going to need Vaseline® to get me out one of these days!"

Impacting the Educational Program

"Tuck helps us provide an educational environment that is secure, safe, and comfortable," says Robert. "As managers, we all share a sense of security knowing that Tuck is available to handle emergent situations that threaten to diminish building services or even close a school facility."

Tuck has respect for his supervisor and director of operations.

"They are great guys to work with, and they made me feel good asking if I would sign up for another fifteen years instead of considering retirement."

Has he considered retiring? "I've thought about it, and someday I will, but I work with a great crew, and I like being here for the kids and their learning."

Read more about Richard "Tuck" Tucker in Chapters 3 and 14.

A Special Tribute

When Sam and I set out to write this book, we wanted to honor those hidden heroes of the school system who often go unnoticed. As we interviewed the support staff, I was reminded of two special support persons in my own teaching career. This book would not be complete without a tribute to Jean Brody and Bill Lemon.

After graduating from college, I quickly discovered that my degree did not teach me how to survive in the real world of education. Fortunately, Jean Brody, an assistant in the Title One program in Henderson, North Carolina, took me under her wing. Jean provided the support and guidance to help me through that first year. Jean lived her faith and taught me more than how to be an educator. I lost contact with Jean more than thirty years ago. I am not sure she ever realized the impact she had on my career and my life. Perhaps this book will make its way into her hands.

When I left the classroom for administration, I again found myself with a new degree but no knowledge about the real world of administration. The first day I walked into Lovettsville Elementary School (Loudoun County, Virginia), Mr. Bill Lemon greeted me. Bill was the head custodian. He took one look at me and knew I was greener than a zucchini.

Bill was proud of our school. He kept the building immaculate and the grounds manicured. He treated the staff like family and always had an encouraging word for students. Bill taught me all the important things about running a school. He made sure I knew how to deactivate the security and fire alarms. He trained me in the virtues of VOBAN® (Aromatic Absorbant). He taught me how to check the circuit box if the ice cream started melting. And he always came to my rescue.

One Saturday, Lovettsville had a fund–raiser barbeque. I was scheduled to make coleslaw at seven AM. Well, about five that morning I had an encounter with a skunk while walking my dog. I changed my clothes, showered and shampooed with tomato juice, sprayed cologne from head to foot, and drove to work with the car windows wide open to air me out even more. Yet when I walked into that building, Bill took one sniff and asked if I had been skunked. Only a good friend loves you enough to ask a question like that! We discovered the source of the smell—I had not changed my shoes, and the crepe soles had absorbed the odor. I threw my shoes and socks into the dumpster and washed my feet with the strongest cleanser I could find in Bill's storage closet.

I did not have time to go home for shoes, so I declared that my bare feet would have to hide under the kitchen counter. (Note to Health Inspectors: I washed both of those feet with chlorine–based cleansers, okay?)

As I scurried about grating the cabbage, Bill disappeared. A few minutes before our parent volunteers arrived, someone tapped me on the shoulder. I turned and saw Bill holding out a pair of flower–printed slippers. He said he purchased them from the drugstore that opened at eight AM in a neighboring town. Bill had convinced the store employees to let him in before opening time so he could get the shoes back to me before anyone caught me bare–footed in the kitchen. I still have those slippers.

Bill did things like that for all the staff members. He washed their coffee cups if they forgot to do so, slipped hard candies onto their desks, carried boxes to their cars, and fixed their flats. All of that in addition to taking care of the building and the grounds so the children would have a clean, safe, and comfortable place to learn. Bill cared about the staff, and he cared about the students.

After Bill retired, he still came to the school every day and brought the mail from the post office box. Then he would mosey down the hall with a pocket full of candy for the teachers and a friendly wave for the students. His last stop would be by my office to see if I needed anything. Bill Lemon, or Mr. Sweet Lemon as I liked to call him, was a friend and a colleague. I could not have been as successful in my job without Bill's advice, encouragement, and support.

So in honor of Jean Brody and in memory of Bill Lemon, I say a heartfelt thank–you to all of the school support persons who read this book. You are appreciated.

–Vie Herlocker

Resources

Support Staff Professional Organizations and Informational Sites

National Education Association. NEA has a division for Educational Support Personnel (ESP), and the monthly journal, *nea today*, has a standing column for support staff issues.
www.nea.org/esphome

National Association for Pupil Transportation
www.napt.org

National Association of Educational Office Professionals
www.naeop.org

National Association of School Nurses
www.nasn.org

US Department of Agriculture—Food and Nutrition Information Center
www.nal.usda.gov/fnic/etext/000041.html

National Resource Center for Paraprofessionals
www.nrcpara.org

General Resource Websites:

Dictionary.com. This Web resource features several dictionaries and a thesaurus, and includes an optional feature for English and/or Spanish "word of the day" sent to your e–mail.
www.dictionary.com

Capital Community College Foundation in Hartford, CT.
Online guide to grammar and writing.
www.grammar.ccc.commnet.edu/grammar/

Internet Public Library
www.ipl.org

Need hints for writing your resume? This free site specializes in the
trade professions.
www.free–resume–tips.com/resumetips/trade.html

Ways to Offer Your Services in the Classroom

If you work in an elementary school, ask your librarian to order
books about your career. Most school librarians welcome order
requests from staff members. Let the teachers know when the books
arrive and offer to visit the classrooms to read to the students and
talk about your job.

If you work in a middle or high school, offer to visit classes for career
day and talk about your job. Your guidance office should have books
and information available for you to share with the older students.

These are a few fun books to consider for the younger students:

Mr. Carillo: The A+ Custodian by Louise Borden. Published in 2004 by
Simon and Shuster.
www.simonsays.com

The Black Lagoon series by Mike Thayer: These funny books will
have the younger kids laughing and give you a chance to answer
questions about what your job really involves.

These books are published by Scholastic Paperbacks. They can be
ordered from Amazon.com. Most likely, these titles are already in
your elementary school and library.

The School Nurse from the Black Lagoon
The Custodian from the Black Lagoon
The School Bus Driver from the Black Lagoon
The Cafeteria Lady from the Black Lagoon
The Principal from the Black Lagoon

Celebrate Yourself

These cartoon books will provide your daily recommended requirements for laughter!

The School Custodian...A Tribute to Those Who Maintain, Enhance, and Spread Sunshine in our Buildings

The School Nurse...A Tribute to Those Who Dispense Wisdom, Encouragement, and TLC!

The School Bus Driver...A Tribute to the Fearless Who Transport and Care for Often Difficult Cargo!

The School Cafeteria Worker...A Tribute to Those Who Nourish, Nurture, and Encourage Young Bodies!

The School Secretary...A Tribute to Those Who Really Run Our Schools

This series is compiled by Dave and Nancy Craig, published 2005. They may be ordered from the publisher:

Paperbacks for Educators
426 West Front Street
Washington, Missouri 63090
800–227–2591
Amazon.com also carries these books.

References

Bartlett, William S. "Three Strategies for Establishing Legendary Customer Service." In *Sizzling Customer Service,* ed. Doug Smart, 15–30. Roswell, GA: James and Brookfield Publishers, 1998.

Bartlett, William S. "Building Blocks for Productive Teams." Sam Bartlett Seminars, 1998.

Bartlett, William S. "How to Handle Conflict and Manage Anger." Sam Bartlett Seminars, 1998.

Bartlett, William S. "How to Communicate with Confidence, Clarity, and Charisma." Sam Bartlett Seminars, 1998.

Bartlett, William S. "Sizzling Customer Service: Principles for Having "More Success with Less Stress." Sam Bartlett Seminars, 2004.

Blanchard, Kenneth H. *We Are the Beloved: A Spiritual Journey.* Grand Rapids, MI: Zondervan, 1994.

Covey, Stephen R., A. Robert Merrill, Rebecca R. Merrill. *First Things First.* New York: Simon and Schuster, 1994.

DiSC Personal Profile System ® 2800, Minneapolis, MN: Inscape Publishing, 1994.

Glasser, William. *Reality Therapy: A New Approach to Psychiatry.* Borgo Press, 1990.

Goleman, Daniel, Richard Boyatzis, Annie McKee. *Primal Leadership.* Boston, MA: Harvard Business School Press, 2002.

Horn, Sam. *Tongue Fu! At School.* Lanham, MD: A Scarecrow Education Book, Taylor Trade Publishing, 2004.

Larson, Val, Mike Carnell. "Surviving Pity City and the Valley of Despair." www.isixsigma.com/library/content/c020812a.asp.

Patterson, Kerry, Joseph Grenny, Ron McMillian, Al Switzler. *Crucial Conversations: Tools for Talking When Stakes Are High.* New York: McGraw Hill, 2000.

professional. Dictionary.com. The American Heritage® Dictionary of the English Language, Fourth Edition. Houghton Mifflin Company, 2004. http://dictionary.reference.com/browse/professional (accessed: January 14, 2008).

Quotations used throughout this book were collected from sources including:

      www.bartleby.com
      www.brainyquote.com
      www.heartquotes.net
      www.thinkexist.com

INDEX

Meet the Authors

SAM BARTLETT

Sam Bartlett is the CEO of Family Friendly Schools (www.familyfriendlyschools.com) and a noted authority in the areas of leadership, team building, communication, and how to provide legendary customer service. He has provided on-site training for numerous school districts, Fortune 500 companies, and government agencies. Participants consistently rank his workshops as "the best they have ever attended."

Before assuming his current position, Mr. Bartlett was CEO of Digital Juice, Inc., an internationally recognized leader in 3-D animation and interactive media. Mr. Bartlett led the company to a record-breaking 300 percent growth his first year by focusing on Customer Service and building a High-Performing Team. Sam lives in Virginia with his wife, Linda, and their five children. (Visit www.engageinstitute.com/sbartlett for more information.)

VIE HERLOCKER

Vie Herlocker is a writer and an educator. She has published in Guideposts, Mature Living, Penned from the Heart, and Miracles of Forgiveness. Her career spanned thirty years as a teacher and elementary school administrator. She also helped in the front office, the clinic, and did her share of bus duty. Vie tackled most custodial jobs that didn't involve electricity, but cafeteria work was her greatest achievement. Although she was banned from experimenting with that humongous mixer, she could serve trays and wash dishes like a pro. (Visit www.engageinstitute.com/vherlocker for more information.)

Printed in the United States
219048BV00003B/2/P

9 780981 454306